the cherokee native american tribe for kids

Journey Through Cherokee History

sarah michaels

Copyright © 2024 by Sarah Michaels

All rights reserved.

No part of this book may be reproduced in any form or by any electronic or mechanical means, including information storage and retrieval systems, without written permission from the author, except for the use of brief quotations in a book review.

contents

Introduction	5
1. THE CHEROKEE LAND	15
Original homeland of the Cherokee	15
Key features of the landscape	18
Early settlements and lifestyle	20
2. DAILY LIFE OF THE CHEROKEE	25
Types of homes (wattle and daub houses)	25
Village life and community structure	27
Traditional Cherokee foods and farming methods	30
Hunting, fishing, and gathering practices	33
Traditional Cherokee clothing and how it was made	36
Importance of beadwork, pottery, and basket weaving	38
3. CULTURE AND TRADITIONS	43
Introduction to the Cherokee language	43
Importance of storytelling	45
Traditional Cherokee music and instruments	48
Types of dances and their significance	51
Major Cherokee festivals and their meanings	54
How these festivals are celebrated	57
4. GOVERNANCE AND SOCIETY	61
Structure of Cherokee leadership and councils	61
Role of chiefs and clan leaders	64
Explanation of the Cherokee clan system	67
Importance of clans in social structure and marriage	70

5. CHEROKEE BELIEFS AND SPIRITUALITY — 75
- Overview of Cherokee spiritual beliefs — 75
- Connection to nature and the land — 78
- Role of medicine men and women — 81
- Traditional healing practices and herbal medicine — 84

6. THE TRAIL OF TEARS — 89
- Events leading up to the Trail of Tears — 89
- Impact of the Indian Removal Act — 92
- Forced relocation — 94
- How the Cherokee rebuilt their communities — 97
- Lasting impact on the Cherokee people — 100

7. MODERN CHEROKEE LIFE — 103
- Life in modern Cherokee communities — 103
- Efforts to preserve and revive Cherokee culture — 106
- Programs to teach Cherokee language and traditions — 110
- Role of schools and cultural centers — 114

8. CHEROKEE CONTRIBUTIONS AND NOTABLE FIGURES — 117
- Profiles of notable Cherokee leaders — 117
- Achievements of Cherokee individuals in various fields — 121

9. ACTIVITIES AND PROJECTS — 127
- Crafts — 127
- Cooking traditional Cherokee recipes — 131
- Basic Cherokee words and phrases — 135

Glosary — 141
Resources — 147
Appendix — 151

introduction

brief overview of who the cherokee are

Imagine waking up to the sound of birds singing in the trees, with the morning sun peeking through the leaves, and the fresh scent of pine in the air. This was the daily life of the Cherokee people, who lived in the southeastern United States long before cars, phones, or even the United States itself existed. The Cherokee, also known as the Tsalagi in their own language, were one of the largest Native American tribes in this region.

The Cherokee are known for their deep connection to the land. They lived in the Appalachian Mountains, a region filled with lush forests, clear rivers, and abundant wildlife. Their villages were often located near rivers, which provided water for drinking, cooking, and farming. The land was not just a place to live but a source of life and spirituality. Every mountain, tree, and river had a story and a spirit.

The homes of the Cherokee were quite different from the houses we live in today. They built sturdy, warm homes from natural materials found in their environment. Their summer homes were made of a wooden frame covered with bark and woven vines, providing a cool shelter during the hot months.

Introduction

In winter, they lived in small, dome-shaped houses called "asi," made from mud and clay plastered over a wooden frame. These homes were designed to keep the cold out and the warmth in, using the natural insulation properties of the earth.

Family and community were at the heart of Cherokee life. Each village was like a big family, with everyone working together and helping each other. The Cherokee had a unique system called the clan system. There were seven clans, each named after animals or natural elements like the Wolf Clan, the Deer Clan, and the Paint Clan. Your clan was like your extended family, and it played a big part in your life. It decided who you could marry, what roles you might take in ceremonies, and how you were connected to others in your village.

The Cherokee people were farmers, hunters, and gatherers. They were known for their "Three Sisters" crops: corn, beans, and squash. These plants were grown together in a way that they helped each other. Corn provided a structure for the beans to climb, beans added nitrogen to the soil, and squash spread along the ground, blocking weeds and keeping the soil moist. This method of farming was not only clever but also ensured a balanced diet.

Hunting was also an important part of Cherokee life. Men would go on hunting trips to catch deer, bear, and wild turkeys, which provided meat for the village. They used bows and arrows, traps, and spears, and they respected the animals they hunted, believing that the spirits of these animals would continue to live on.

Cherokee culture was rich with stories, songs, and dances. Storytelling was a way to pass down history, traditions, and lessons from one generation to the next. One famous story is about the first fire. It tells how the animals worked together to bring fire to the Cherokee people, each animal facing challenges along the way. These stories were often told by the elders, who were respected for their wisdom and knowledge.

Introduction

Music and dance were also important. The Cherokee played flutes, drums, and rattles, creating music that accompanied their dances. Each dance had a special meaning and was performed at ceremonies and festivals. For example, the Stomp Dance was a social dance that brought the community together. People danced in a circle, moving to the rhythm of the music, with everyone participating, young and old alike.

One of the most significant aspects of Cherokee life was their belief system and spirituality. They believed in a Great Spirit who created the world and everything in it. They also believed in many other spirits that inhabited the natural world. These spirits could be found in animals, plants, and even the weather. The Cherokee people had ceremonies to honor these spirits and to ask for their help and guidance. One important ceremony was the Green Corn Ceremony, a thanksgiving celebration held when the corn was ready to harvest. It was a time of renewal, forgiveness, and giving thanks for the harvest.

The Cherokee were not just skilled farmers and hunters; they were also talented artisans. They made beautiful pottery, baskets, and beadwork. Their pottery was both functional and decorative, used for cooking, storing food, and serving meals. The baskets, woven from river cane, white oak, or honeysuckle, were used for gathering crops, carrying goods, and even for ceremonial purposes. Beadwork was used to decorate clothing, bags, and other items, often in intricate patterns that had special meanings.

In addition to their crafts, the Cherokee were known for their unique written language, developed by a Cherokee man named Sequoyah in the early 19th century. Sequoyah saw the value of written communication and created a syllabary, a set of written symbols that represent syllables. This allowed the Cherokee people to read and write in their own language, preserving their stories, laws, and knowledge in a new way. The Cherokee syllabary was one of the first writing systems

Introduction

created by a Native American tribe and remains an important part of Cherokee culture today.

Despite their rich culture and strong community, the Cherokee faced many challenges, especially during the 19th century. The arrival of European settlers brought significant changes and difficulties. The Cherokee tried to adapt by adopting some European customs and ways of life, such as farming techniques and education systems. However, their land was highly desired by settlers, leading to conflicts and forced removals.

One of the most tragic events in Cherokee history is the Trail of Tears. In the 1830s, the U.S. government forcibly removed the Cherokee from their homeland, pushing them to march over a thousand miles to what is now Oklahoma. Many Cherokee people suffered and died during this journey. Despite this hardship, the Cherokee showed incredible resilience. They rebuilt their communities, continued their traditions, and maintained their identity.

Today, the Cherokee people are divided into three federally recognized tribes: the Eastern Band of Cherokee Indians in North Carolina, the Cherokee Nation, and the United Keetoowah Band of Cherokee Indians, both located in Oklahoma. They work hard to preserve their culture, language, and traditions. Cherokee schools teach the language and history, ensuring that new generations can carry forward their heritage. Festivals and cultural events celebrate Cherokee traditions, keeping the spirit of their ancestors alive.

importance of learning about native american tribes

Why is it so important to learn about these tribes?

First, learning about Native American tribes helps us appreciate the diversity and richness of cultures. The Cherokee, for example, have a fascinating history filled with unique traditions, stories, and ways of life. By exploring their culture, we see how different people can have different ways of living and yet still share common values like community, respect for nature, and storytelling. This appreciation for diversity helps us understand that there isn't just one way to live or one way to see the world. It shows us that there are many different perspectives, each offering valuable lessons and insights.

Understanding Native American tribes also teaches us about respect and empathy. The Cherokee, like many other tribes, have faced significant challenges and injustices, especially during events like the Trail of Tears. By learning about these difficult parts of history, we can develop a deeper empathy for the struggles of others. We learn to respect their strength and resilience in the face of adversity. This respect and empathy are important because they help us become more compassionate and understanding people. They teach us to stand up against injustice and to support those who have been treated unfairly.

Another reason to learn about Native American tribes is to recognize their contributions to our world. The Cherokee, for example, made significant advancements in agriculture with their "Three Sisters" farming method. They also created a unique written language, thanks to Sequoyah's syllabary. These contributions have had a lasting impact and show that Native American tribes were innovative and resourceful. By acknowledging these contributions, we give credit where it's due and ensure that the achievements of Native American people are remembered and celebrated.

Learning about Native American tribes also helps us understand the importance of preserving cultures and languages. Many Native American languages, including Cherokee, are endangered because fewer people speak them today. By studying these languages and supporting efforts to keep them alive, we help preserve a vital part of human heritage. Language is more than just words; it's a way of thinking and seeing the world. When we lose a language, we lose a unique perspective and the wisdom that comes with it.

Introduction

Moreover, studying Native American tribes teaches us about the deep connection between people and the environment. The Cherokee, for example, have always had a strong relationship with the land. They believed that everything in nature had a spirit and that it was important to live in harmony with the natural world. This respect for nature is something we can all learn from, especially as we face environmental challenges today. By understanding how the Cherokee and other tribes lived sustainably, we can find inspiration and guidance for taking better care of our planet.

Another important aspect of learning about Native American tribes is the opportunity to correct misunderstandings and stereotypes. For a long time, Native American people have been portrayed inaccurately in movies, books, and media. These portrayals often show them in a negative or simplistic light, which is unfair and untrue. By learning about the real history and culture of tribes like the Cherokee, we can challenge these stereotypes and promote a more accurate and respectful understanding. This helps create a more inclusive and fair society where everyone's story is valued and respected.

Education about Native American tribes also helps us see the interconnectedness of human history. The story of the Cherokee is not just their story; it's a part of American history and, by extension, world history. Their interactions with European settlers, their forced removal, and their resilience in rebuilding their communities are all parts of a larger narrative that has shaped the world we live in today. By understanding these connections, we can see how different events and cultures influence each other and contribute to the bigger picture.

Lastly, learning about Native American tribes like the Cherokee is a way of honoring their legacy. The Cherokee people have shown incredible strength and resilience over the centuries. Despite the many challenges they faced, they have kept their culture, traditions, and identity alive. By learning about them, we show respect for their journey and their contributions. We help ensure that their story is not forgotten but remembered and celebrated for generations to come.

overview of what will be covered in the book

Our journey begins by immersing ourselves in the Cherokee homeland. The Cherokee lived in the southeastern United States, a region rich in natural beauty with its rolling mountains, clear rivers, and dense forests. Imagine waking up to the sound of birds singing and the rustling of leaves in the wind. The Cherokee's connection to this land was profound. They didn't just live on it; they lived with it, respecting and honoring every aspect of their environment. We'll explore how the land shaped their daily lives, from the foods they ate to the homes they built.

Speaking of homes, the Cherokee had ingenious ways of constructing their dwellings to suit the changing seasons. Their summer homes, made of woven vines and bark, provided cool shelter during the hot months. When winter arrived, they moved into cozy, dome-shaped houses called "asi," made from mud and clay. These homes kept the cold out and warmth in, creating a snug environment for families. You'll get to see how these homes were built and what life was like inside them.

Family and community were at the heart of Cherokee life. Imagine living in a village where everyone knows each other, helps each other, and celebrates together. The Cherokee had a unique social structure called the clan system. There were seven clans, each with its own name, like the Wolf Clan and the Deer Clan. Your clan was like your extended family, influencing who you could marry and how you connected with others. We'll delve into the roles and responsibilities within this system, showing how it fostered a strong sense of belonging and unity.

The Cherokee were masterful farmers, hunters, and gatherers. They developed a clever method of farming known as the "Three Sisters," where corn, beans, and squash were grown together. This method not only produced a bountiful harvest but also ensured the plants supported each other's growth. Imagine planting seeds in the rich soil and watching them grow into tall corn stalks, climbing beans, and sprawling squash vines. We'll explore the tools and techniques they used and how they hunted animals like deer and wild turkeys for food.

Storytelling was an essential part of Cherokee culture. Through stories, they passed down their history, beliefs, and values from one generation to the next. Picture sitting around a fire, listening to an elder tell the tale of how fire was brought to the Cherokee people. These stories were more than just entertainment; they were a way of preserving knowledge and teaching important lessons. You'll get to hear some of these fascinating legends and understand their significance.

Music and dance were also integral to Cherokee life. They used flutes, drums, and rattles to create music that accompanied their dances. Each dance had a special meaning, often connected to nature or spiritual beliefs. Imagine joining in a Stomp Dance, moving in a circle to the rhythmic beat of the drums, feeling the energy and connection with the community. We'll explore the different types of dances and the occasions they were performed, showing how they brought people together and celebrated their heritage.

Spirituality and beliefs were deeply woven into the fabric of Cherokee life. They believed in a Great Spirit who created the world and many other spirits inhabiting the natural world. Imagine walking through a forest and feeling the presence of these spirits in the trees, animals, and even the weather. The Cherokee held ceremonies to honor these spirits and seek their guidance. One such ceremony was the Green Corn Ceremony, a time of thanksgiving and renewal. We'll learn about these spiritual practices and how they influenced daily life and decision-making.

Despite their rich culture and strong community, the Cherokee faced many challenges, especially with the arrival of European settlers. These encounters brought significant changes and hardships, culminating in the tragic Trail of Tears. Imagine being forced to leave your home and walk over a thousand miles to a new, unfamiliar land. Many Cherokee suffered and died during this journey, yet their resilience and strength shone through as they rebuilt their communities. We'll examine this difficult period and how the Cherokee overcame it, showing their determination to preserve their way of life.

Today, the Cherokee people continue to honor their traditions while embracing modern life. There are three federally recognized Cherokee tribes: the Eastern Band of Cherokee Indians in North Carolina, the Cherokee Nation, and the United Keetoowah Band of Cherokee Indians in Oklahoma. These communities work hard to keep their culture and language alive. Imagine visiting a Cherokee school where children learn to speak their ancestral language and practice traditional crafts. We'll see how these efforts ensure that Cherokee heritage is passed on to future generations.

The story of the Cherokee is not just a tale of the past; it's a living, evolving narrative that continues to inspire and teach us. By learning about the Cherokee, we gain a deeper understanding of the diverse threads that make up the fabric of our world. Their history, culture, and contributions enrich our collective story, reminding us of the importance of respect, resilience, and community.

As we journey through the chapters of this book, you'll find yourself stepping into the shoes of the Cherokee people, experiencing their world through their eyes. You'll see how their traditions and beliefs are not just relics of the past but living practices that continue to shape their identity and values. Each section will bring you closer to understanding the Cherokee way of life, from their innovative farming techniques to their spiritual ceremonies and everything in between.

Introduction

By the end of our journey, you'll have a deeper appreciation for the Cherokee and their enduring legacy. You'll understand why it's so important to learn about Native American tribes and how their stories contribute to our shared human experience. Through their resilience and wisdom, the Cherokee people offer valuable lessons that resonate across time and space, teaching us about the power of community, the importance of preserving our heritage, and the beauty of living in harmony with nature.

So get ready to embark on this adventure, exploring the rich tapestry of Cherokee culture and history. As we travel through time, you'll discover the many ways in which the Cherokee have shaped and continue to influence the world around us. Their story is a testament to the strength of the human spirit and the enduring power of tradition and community.

1 /
the cherokee land

original homeland of the cherokee

THE LANDSCAPE of the Cherokee homeland is varied and rich. There are tall, majestic mountains covered in thick forests of oak, pine, and hickory trees. The forests were like a giant pantry, providing the Cherokee with everything they needed. They gathered nuts, berries, and herbs, and hunted deer, turkey, and other animals that roamed these woods. Imagine walking through these forests, the air filled with the scent of pine and the sounds of birds singing overhead. The Cherokee knew every inch of these woods, and they had deep respect for the animals and plants that lived there.

Running through this mountainous region are clear, fast-flowing rivers and streams. Rivers like the Tennessee, Hiwassee, and Oconaluftee were vital to the Cherokee way of life. These waterways were their highways, used for travel and trade. The rivers provided fresh water for drinking and cooking, and they were full of fish like trout and bass, which were important sources of food. Picture a group of Cherokee children playing by the river, skipping stones across the water, while the adults fish or paddle their canoes downstream.

The valleys between the mountains were fertile and lush, perfect for farming. This is where the Cherokee planted their crops. They used a method called "Three Sisters" farming, growing corn, beans, and squash together. This clever technique allowed the plants to support each other. The corn stalks provided a structure for the beans to climb, the beans added nutrients to the soil, and the squash spread out along the ground, keeping weeds at bay and retaining moisture in the soil. Imagine fields of green corn stalks swaying in the breeze, beans twining up their stems, and bright orange squash flowers blooming beneath.

The climate of the Cherokee homeland was mild, with warm summers and cool winters. This allowed for a long growing season, which meant the Cherokee could harvest plenty of food to sustain them through the year. In the summer, they enjoyed the warmth and sunshine, spending time outdoors and tending to their crops. In the winter, they moved into their cozy, mud-and-clay homes, staying warm and safe from the cold. The changing seasons brought different activities and rhythms to their lives, from planting and harvesting to hunting and gathering.

One of the most striking features of the Cherokee homeland is its natural beauty. The Blue Ridge Mountains, part of the larger Appalachian range, are famous for their stunning vistas and biodiversity. The mountains get their name from the bluish haze that often surrounds them, giving them a magical, otherworldly appearance. This haze is caused by the trees releasing natural oils into the air, which scatter blue light.

Imagine standing on a mountain peak, looking out over a sea of blue-green hills, with the sky above and the world stretching out below. For the Cherokee, these mountains were more than just a backdrop; they were sacred places, filled with stories and spirits.

The Cherokee had a deep spiritual connection to their homeland. They believed that the land was a living entity, with its own spirits and powers. They performed ceremonies and rituals to honor these spirits, asking for their blessings and guidance. Sacred sites like the Kituwah Mound, considered the mother town of the Cherokee, were places of great spiritual significance. These places were where they held important ceremonies, made decisions for the tribe, and connected with their ancestors. Imagine gathering around a sacred fire, the flames dancing in the night, as the elders tell stories of the Great Spirit and the creation of the world.

The natural resources of the Cherokee homeland also played a crucial role in their daily lives. The forests provided wood for building homes and making tools, while the rivers supplied clay for pottery and stones for weapons. The Cherokee were skilled artisans, creating beautiful and functional items from the materials around them. They made pottery for cooking and storage, baskets for gathering food, and intricate beadwork for clothing and decoration. Picture a Cherokee woman weaving a basket from river cane, her hands moving quickly and skillfully, creating a pattern that has been passed down through generations.

The land was also a place of learning and discovery for the Cherokee children. They learned to hunt, fish, and farm from their parents and grandparents. They were taught to read the signs of nature, understanding the movements of animals, the growth of plants, and the changing weather. This knowledge was essential for survival and was passed down through stories, songs, and hands-on experience. Imagine a young Cherokee boy following his father through the forest, learning to track a deer, or a girl helping her mother in the fields, planting seeds and tending to the crops.

key features of the landscape

Let's dive into these key features of the Cherokee landscape and see how they shaped the lives and culture of the Cherokee people.

First, let's talk about the mountains. The Appalachian Mountains, where the Cherokee lived, are among the oldest mountain ranges in the world. These mountains are not just towering peaks; they are rolling, verdant hills covered in dense forests. Picture yourself standing on a mountaintop, looking out over a sea of green that stretches to the horizon. The mountains are alive with the sounds of birds, the rustling of leaves, and the whisper of the wind. For the Cherokee, these mountains were more than just a backdrop; they were a source of life, providing shelter, food, and spiritual connection.

The Blue Ridge Mountains, part of the Appalachian range, are especially stunning. They get their name from the bluish haze that often surrounds them. This haze is caused by the trees releasing natural oils into the air, which scatter blue light. Imagine looking out over the Blue Ridge Mountains on a sunny day, the haze giving the landscape a magical, dreamlike quality. The Cherokee believed that these mountains were inhabited by spirits and held great spiritual significance. They performed ceremonies and rituals to honor these spirits and seek their guidance.

Moving on from the mountains, let's explore the rivers that flow through the Cherokee homeland. Rivers like the Tennessee, Hiwassee, and Oconaluftee were the lifeblood of the Cherokee people. These rivers provided fresh water for drinking, cooking, and farming. They were also filled with fish, which were an important source of food. Imagine sitting by the riverbank, watching the water sparkle in the sunlight as fish swim beneath the surface. The Cherokee used canoes to travel up and down these rivers, trading goods and connecting with other villages. These waterways were like natural highways, making travel and communication easier.

The rivers were also places of beauty and tranquility. Imagine a group of Cherokee children playing by the river, skipping stones across the water, while adults fish or paddle their canoes. The sounds of laughter mix with the gentle murmur of the river, creating a peaceful and joyful atmosphere. The rivers were not just practical resources; they were places of relaxation and connection with nature.

Now, let's venture into the forests that covered much of the Cherokee homeland. These forests were rich and diverse, filled with towering trees, lush undergrowth, and a variety of wildlife. Imagine walking through a dense forest, the ground covered in a soft carpet of leaves and pine needles. Sunlight filters through the canopy, casting dappled shadows on the forest floor. The air is filled with the scent of pine, the songs of birds, and the rustling of small animals in the underbrush.

. . .

Sarah Michaels

The Cherokee relied on these forests for many of their daily needs. They gathered nuts, berries, and herbs for food and medicine. They hunted deer, turkey, and other animals for meat. The forests provided wood for building homes and making tools. Imagine a Cherokee hunter moving silently through the forest, tracking a deer, or a woman gathering wild berries in a woven basket. The forests were like a giant pantry and pharmacy, offering everything the Cherokee needed to survive and thrive.

The forests were also places of spiritual significance. The Cherokee believed that every tree, plant, and animal had a spirit. They performed ceremonies to honor these spirits and ensure harmony with the natural world. Imagine a group of Cherokee people gathered in a forest clearing, singing and dancing around a sacred fire. The flames flicker and dance, casting a warm glow on the faces of the participants. These ceremonies were a way to connect with the spirits of the forest and seek their blessings.

One particularly important tree for the Cherokee was the white oak. Its strong, durable wood was used to build homes, tools, and canoes. The acorns from the white oak were gathered and processed into flour, providing a valuable food source. Imagine the process of gathering acorns, removing their shells, and grinding them into flour using stone tools. This was a communal activity, with families working together to prepare food for the winter.

early settlements and lifestyle

Cherokee villages were carefully planned and built to suit the needs of the community. Picture a collection of homes made from natural materials like wood, mud, and clay. These homes were built to be both functional and comfortable, providing shelter from the elements. In the summer, families lived in open, airy structures made from a framework of wooden poles covered with woven vines and bark. These summer homes were cool and allowed air to flow freely, making them perfect for the hot months.

As winter approached, the Cherokee moved into their "asi" or winter homes. These were small, dome-shaped structures made from a wooden frame covered with a thick layer of mud and clay. The design of these homes helped keep the cold out and the warmth in, creating a snug environment during the colder months. Imagine the coziness of a winter home, with a fire burning in the center, providing warmth and light as families gathered together.

The heart of the village was often the council house, a large, round structure where important meetings and ceremonies took place. The council house was a symbol of the community's unity and cooperation. Here, leaders and elders gathered to discuss important matters, make decisions, and hold ceremonies. Picture the council house filled with people, the air buzzing with conversation as decisions are made that will affect the entire village.

Daily life in a Cherokee village was a blend of work, play, and community activities. Men and women had different roles, each contributing to the well-being of the village. The men were responsible for hunting, fishing, and protecting the community. They would venture into the forests and rivers to provide food, using their skills and knowledge of the land to track and hunt animals like deer and wild turkeys. Imagine a group of hunters returning to the village with their catch, greeted by the excited chatter of children and the proud smiles of their families.

Women, on the other hand, were in charge of farming, gathering, and managing the household. They cultivated the fields, growing the "Three Sisters" crops—corn, beans, and squash. These crops were essential to the Cherokee diet and were planted in a way that allowed them to support each other's growth. Imagine the women working together in the fields, their hands moving skillfully as they plant seeds and tend to the crops. They also gathered wild fruits, nuts, and medicinal herbs from the forests, ensuring that the village had a diverse and balanced diet.

Children in the village learned by watching and helping their parents. They were taught the skills they would need as adults through hands-on experience and storytelling. Boys learned to hunt and fish, practicing with small bows and arrows, while girls helped their mothers in the fields and learned to weave baskets and make pottery. Picture a group of children playing games that mimic the activities of the adults, their laughter ringing out as they learn and grow.

The Cherokee had a rich tradition of storytelling, music, and dance. These cultural activities were woven into the fabric of daily life and were a way to pass down history, values, and lessons from one generation to the next. In the evenings, families would gather around the fire to listen to stories told by the elders. These stories often featured animals and spirits and taught important lessons about respect, bravery, and community. Imagine the flickering light of the fire casting shadows as an elder tells a story, the children listening with wide eyes, captivated by the tales of their ancestors.

. . .

Music and dance were also integral to Cherokee life. They used flutes, drums, and rattles to create music that accompanied their dances. Each dance had a special meaning and was performed at different times of the year. The Stomp Dance, for example, was a social dance that brought the community together. Participants danced in a circle, moving to the rhythm of the music, with everyone from the youngest child to the oldest elder joining in. Imagine the joyful sounds of the music and the sight of the dancers moving in unison, their feet stamping the ground in a rhythmic beat.

Ceremonies and festivals were important events in the Cherokee calendar. These gatherings were times of celebration, reflection, and renewal. The Green Corn Ceremony, held when the corn was ready to harvest, was one of the most important. It was a time to give thanks for the harvest, to forgive past wrongs, and to start anew. Imagine the village coming together for this ceremony, the air filled with the scent of roasting corn, the sounds of songs and prayers, and the sense of unity and gratitude.

The Cherokee were also skilled artisans, creating beautiful and functional items from the materials around them. They made pottery for cooking and storage, baskets for gathering food, and intricate beadwork for clothing and decoration. Each piece was crafted with care and skill, often featuring patterns and designs that held special meanings. Imagine a Cherokee woman carefully weaving a basket, her hands moving deftly as she creates a work of art that will be used in daily life.

. . .

Sarah Michaels

Trade was another important aspect of Cherokee life. They traded goods with neighboring tribes and later with European settlers. This exchange of goods allowed them to acquire items that were not available in their homeland, such as metal tools and woven cloth. Imagine a bustling trading scene, with people exchanging goods, sharing news, and building relationships with others from different communities.

2 / daily life of the cherokee

types of homes (wattle and daub houses)

WATTLE and daub houses were common in many Cherokee villages. The construction of these homes involved weaving a framework of wooden sticks, or wattle, and then covering this framework with a mixture of mud, clay, and straw, known as daub. This combination created walls that were both strong and insulating, perfect for the varying weather conditions in the Appalachian region. Imagine the skill and effort that went into building these homes, with each step reflecting the Cherokee's deep connection to the land and their understanding of natural materials.

The first step in building a wattle and daub house was to gather the materials. The Cherokee would collect flexible saplings and branches from the forest to create the wattle. These branches were carefully chosen for their strength and flexibility, making them ideal for weaving. Picture a group of Cherokee men and women walking through the forest, selecting the best branches and carrying them back to the village. This task required knowledge of the different types of trees and their properties, a knowledge passed down through generations.

Sarah Michaels

Once the materials were gathered, the construction of the framework began. The wattle was created by weaving the branches in and out of upright stakes that were firmly planted in the ground. This weaving process created a sturdy lattice that formed the skeleton of the walls. Imagine the careful hands of the builders as they weave the branches, ensuring that each piece is secure and in place. The result was a strong and flexible framework that could withstand the elements.

Next came the application of the daub. The Cherokee mixed mud, clay, and straw to create a thick, sticky plaster. This mixture was then smeared over the wattle framework, filling in the gaps and creating a solid wall. Imagine children and adults working together, their hands covered in mud as they smooth the daub over the walls. This part of the process was not only practical but also a communal activity that brought the village together. The daub would dry and harden, creating a durable and weather-resistant surface.

The roof of a wattle and daub house was just as important as the walls. The Cherokee used thatch, which is made from dried grasses, reeds, or bark, to cover the roof. This material was layered thickly to provide insulation and protection from rain. Imagine the roof being constructed, layer by layer, with careful attention to ensure that it would keep out the rain and snow. The thatched roof was lightweight yet effective, perfectly suited to the structure of the house.

Inside a wattle and daub house, the space was cozy and functional. The floor was often made of packed earth, which was cool in the summer and warm in the winter. The central feature of the home was a fire pit, which provided heat and a place to cook. Imagine the warm glow of the fire, casting flickering shadows on the walls as a family gathered around to share a meal and tell stories. The smoke from the fire would escape through a hole in the roof, keeping the air inside clear and breathable.

The design of wattle and daub houses varied depending on the needs of the family and the resources available. Some homes were round, while others were rectangular. The size of the house could also vary, with larger homes accommodating extended families. Imagine walking through a village and seeing a variety of home shapes and sizes, each one reflecting the unique needs and preferences of its inhabitants.

One of the remarkable aspects of wattle and daub construction was its sustainability. The materials used were all natural and locally sourced, meaning that the impact on the environment was minimal. When a house was no longer needed or fell into disrepair, it would naturally decompose, leaving no harmful waste behind. This harmony with the environment was a key aspect of Cherokee life, reflecting their respect for the land and its resources.

Living in wattle and daub houses also influenced the social dynamics of the Cherokee village. These homes were close together, creating a tight-knit community where people could easily interact and support one another. Imagine children running between houses, playing games and learning from their elders, or adults gathering to share news and help each other with daily tasks. This sense of community was strengthened by the physical closeness of their homes.

The wattle and daub houses were not just places to live; they were symbols of the Cherokee's ingenuity and connection to their environment. They represented a way of life that was deeply rooted in the natural world, where every material was used thoughtfully and every home was built with care. These houses were warm in the winter, cool in the summer, and able to withstand the changing seasons, providing a comfortable and safe space for Cherokee families.

village life and community structure

The layout of a Cherokee village was both practical and symbolic. At the center of the village was the council house, a large, round building where important meetings and ceremonies took place. This central location reflected the council

Sarah Michaels

house's importance as the heart of the community. Imagine walking through the village and seeing people heading to the council house to discuss matters of governance, celebrate festivals, or resolve conflicts. The council house was a place of gathering, where the voices of the people could be heard and respected.

Surrounding the council house were the homes of the villagers, arranged in clusters that represented the various clans within the tribe. Each clan was an extended family group, and living close together helped to strengthen familial bonds. The Cherokee had a matrilineal system, which meant that clan membership was passed down through the mother. Imagine a child growing up surrounded by aunts, uncles, cousins, and grandparents, all part of the same clan, all contributing to the child's upbringing and education.

The Cherokee were organized into seven clans: Wolf, Deer, Bird, Long Hair, Wild Potato, Blue, and Paint. Each clan had its own specific roles and responsibilities within the village. For example, the Wolf Clan was known for its leadership and often provided the village chiefs. The Deer Clan was associated with hunting and outdoor skills. Imagine the pride a young boy might feel when he learns that he belongs to the Deer Clan and starts to learn the skills and traditions of hunting from his elders.

Daily life in the village was a mix of work, play, and communal activities. Early in the morning, you might see women heading to the fields to tend to the crops. The Cherokee were skilled farmers, and their fields were filled with corn, beans, squash, and other vegetables. These crops were vital to their diet and were cultivated using sustainable practices that had been passed down through generations. Picture the women working together, their hands moving deftly as they plant, weed, and harvest, all the while chatting and sharing stories.

Men, on the other hand, might be preparing for a hunting trip or working on building and repairing tools and structures.

Hunting was not just about providing food; it was also a way to maintain a connection with nature and the spirits of the animals. Imagine a group of men setting out at dawn, their bows and arrows ready, moving silently through the forest as they track deer or wild turkeys. The hunt required skill, patience, and respect for the animals, reflecting the Cherokee's deep spiritual connection to the land.

Children in the village had an important role as well. They were active participants in daily life, learning by observing and helping the adults. From a young age, children were taught the skills they would need as they grew older. Boys learned to hunt and fish, while girls learned to farm, cook, and make crafts. Imagine a group of children playing games that mimic adult activities, such as pretending to hunt or cook, all the while learning valuable lessons through play. These games were not only fun but also educational, preparing the children for their future roles in the community.

Elders held a special place in Cherokee society. They were the keepers of knowledge, history, and tradition. Their wisdom was highly respected, and they played a crucial role in teaching the younger generations. Imagine an elder sitting by the fire in the evening, surrounded by children and adults, telling stories of the past. These stories were more than just entertainment; they were a way to pass down important cultural values and lessons. The elders' tales of bravery, wisdom, and respect for nature helped to shape the moral and ethical framework of the community.

The communal spirit of the village extended to all aspects of life. When it came time to build a new home or repair an existing one, the entire community would come together to help. This cooperative effort was known as a "work party," and it was a time of great camaraderie and shared purpose. Imagine the village buzzing with activity as people gather materials, weave wattle, and apply daub to the walls. The work was accompanied by laughter, songs, and the satisfaction of working together towards a common goal.

Festivals and ceremonies were important events in village life, bringing everyone together to celebrate and honor their traditions. The Green Corn Ceremony, for instance, was a major event that marked the beginning of the corn harvest. It was a time of thanksgiving, renewal, and community bonding. Imagine the village coming alive with music, dance, and feasting, everyone participating in the celebrations. These ceremonies were not just about honoring the harvest; they were also about reaffirming the community's connection to each other and to the land.

The Cherokee's community structure also included a system of governance that was both democratic and inclusive. Each village had a council made up of representatives from each clan. This council made decisions on behalf of the village, ensuring that the voices of all clans were heard. The council was led by a chief, who was chosen based on qualities of leadership, wisdom, and bravery. Imagine a council meeting in progress, with representatives discussing issues, debating solutions, and making decisions that would benefit the entire village.

Conflict resolution was an important aspect of village governance. The Cherokee had a system in place to address disputes and ensure justice. Disputes were often resolved through mediation and consensus, rather than through punishment. Imagine two villagers in conflict, sitting down with a mediator who listens to both sides and helps them find a fair and peaceful resolution. This approach helped to maintain harmony and strengthen the bonds within the community.

traditional cherokee foods and farming methods

The cornerstone of Cherokee agriculture was the "Three Sisters" method, a technique that involved growing corn, beans, and squash together in the same plot. This method was not only efficient but also environmentally sustainable. Each of the "sisters" played a unique role that supported the others. Imagine a field of tall corn stalks standing proudly in the sunlight. These corn stalks provided a natural trellis for the beans to climb, ensuring that the beans received ample sunlight and air circulation.

Meanwhile, the beans enriched the soil by fixing nitrogen, a vital nutrient for plant growth. Picture the beans winding their way up the corn stalks, their green leaves and pods adding to the lushness of the field. At the base of the corn and beans, the squash plants spread out, their large leaves covering the ground. This natural ground cover helped to retain soil moisture and prevent weeds from taking over. The squash leaves created a living mulch, keeping the soil cool and reducing the need for frequent watering.

This harmonious trio of crops—corn, beans, and squash—provided a balanced diet for the Cherokee. Corn, or maize, was a staple food and could be prepared in numerous ways. It was ground into flour to make cornbread, a delicious and filling dish that was often served with meals. Corn was also boiled or roasted and eaten on the cob, just like we enjoy it today. Imagine biting into a fresh ear of roasted corn, the kernels sweet and juicy.

Beans were another important part of the Cherokee diet. They were eaten fresh when in season or dried and stored for use throughout the year. Beans provided a valuable source of protein, which was especially important for a primarily plant-based diet. Imagine a pot of beans simmering over an open fire, the aroma filling the air as the beans cook to perfection. These beans could be mixed with corn and other ingredients to create hearty stews and soups.

Squash, the third sister, came in many varieties, including summer and winter squash. Summer squash was eaten fresh, while winter squash was stored for use during the colder months. The flesh of the squash was rich in vitamins and minerals, making it a nutritious addition to the Cherokee diet.

Sarah Michaels

Imagine the vibrant orange flesh of a butternut squash, sliced and roasted until tender, its natural sweetness enhanced by the heat of the fire.

In addition to the Three Sisters, the Cherokee cultivated a variety of other crops. Sunflowers were grown not only for their seeds, which were eaten as snacks or ground into meal, but also for their oil, which was used in cooking. Picture a field of sunflowers, their bright yellow faces turned towards the sun, adding a splash of color to the landscape.

Tobacco was another important crop, used in both daily life and ceremonial practices. The leaves were dried and could be smoked or used in various rituals. The cultivation of tobacco required careful attention, as it was a valuable and respected plant. Imagine the careful hands of a Cherokee farmer tending to the tobacco plants, ensuring they grow strong and healthy.

The Cherokee also gathered wild foods to supplement their diet. They foraged for nuts, berries, and fruits in the forests surrounding their villages. Hickory nuts, walnuts, and acorns were collected and processed into flour or eaten as snacks. Imagine the taste of freshly gathered hickory nuts, their rich, buttery flavor a delightful treat. Berries such as strawberries, blackberries, and blueberries were picked in season and enjoyed fresh or dried for later use. These wild foods added variety and nutrition to the Cherokee diet.

Hunting and fishing were also crucial components of Cherokee food practices. Men would hunt deer, turkey, and other game animals, using bows and arrows or traps. The meat from these animals was a valuable source of protein and was often smoked or dried to preserve it for later use. Imagine a successful hunting trip, with hunters returning to the village carrying their catch, ready to be shared with their families and neighbors.

Fishing was another important activity, with rivers and streams providing an abundant supply of fish. The Cherokee used various techniques to catch fish, including nets, traps, and fishing lines. Fish were often cooked over an open fire or dried for storage. Picture a family by the river, casting their nets and pulling in a fresh catch, their laughter and excitement echoing along the water's edge.

The agricultural practices of the Cherokee were not just about growing food; they were deeply tied to their cultural and spiritual beliefs. They performed ceremonies to honor the spirits of the crops and to give thanks for a successful harvest. One such ceremony was the Green Corn Ceremony, a major event that marked the beginning of the corn harvest. This ceremony was a time of thanksgiving, renewal, and purification, and it brought the entire community together in celebration.

Imagine the village bustling with activity as preparations for the Green Corn Ceremony begin. People gather in the central plaza, dressed in their finest clothes, ready to participate in the dances, songs, and rituals that honor the spirits of the corn. The air is filled with the sound of drums and the scent of roasting corn, as everyone joins in the festivities, giving thanks for the bountiful harvest and reaffirming their connection to the land.

hunting, fishing, and gathering practices

Hunting required skill, patience, and knowledge of the land. The Cherokee were expert hunters, using a variety of techniques and tools to catch their prey. Imagine a group of hunters quietly moving through the forest, their eyes sharp and their movements silent. They carried bows and arrows, carefully crafted from wood and stone, designed for accuracy and power. These bows were often made from hickory or black locust wood, known for their strength and flexibility.

The hunters tracked deer, turkey, and other game animals, reading the signs of the forest to find their quarry. Imagine the hunters stopping to examine a set of tracks, discussing the age and direction of the animal. They used their knowledge of animal behavior and the landscape to predict where the game would go. This required not only physical skill but also a deep understanding of nature.

When a hunter spotted a deer, he would draw his bow slowly and quietly, aiming carefully before releasing the arrow. The goal was to make a clean, swift kill, respecting the animal and ensuring that no part of it went to waste. The meat was used for food, the hides for clothing and shelter, and the bones for tools and ornaments. Imagine the satisfaction of a successful hunt, knowing that the effort would sustain the village through the seasons.

Fishing was another vital activity for the Cherokee, who lived near rivers and streams teeming with fish. Fishing techniques varied depending on the location and the type of fish being caught. The Cherokee used nets, traps, and fishing lines made from natural fibers. Picture a group of people along the riverbank, casting their nets into the water and pulling them back, filled with fish.

One effective method was the use of fish weirs, structures built from stones or wooden stakes placed in the river to guide fish into traps. These weirs were ingeniously designed to take advantage of the natural flow of the river, making it easier to catch large quantities of fish. Imagine constructing a fish weir, carefully placing each stone or stake to ensure it would hold against the current and guide the fish into the trap.

Fishing was often a communal activity, with men, women, and children all participating. The catch was shared among the village, providing a vital source of protein. Fish could be eaten fresh or dried and smoked for preservation. Imagine the smoky scent of fish drying over a fire, a method that allowed the Cherokee to store food for the winter months.

Gathering was equally important, as the forests and fields provided a wealth of edible plants, nuts, and berries. The Cherokee had an extensive knowledge of the plants in their environment, understanding which ones were edible, medicinal, or useful for other purposes. Imagine a group of women and children walking through the forest, baskets in hand, as they gather nuts, berries, and wild herbs.

Nuts like hickory nuts, walnuts, and acorns were abundant in the Cherokee homeland. These nuts were collected and processed into flour or eaten as snacks. Picture the process of gathering acorns, removing their shells, and leaching them to remove the bitter tannins, transforming them into a nutritious food source. This knowledge of plant processing was passed down through generations, ensuring that the community could make the most of the natural resources available to them.

Berries such as strawberries, blackberries, and blueberries were gathered in season and enjoyed fresh or dried for later use. These berries added variety and nutrition to the Cherokee diet. Imagine the joy of finding a patch of ripe strawberries, their bright red fruits gleaming in the sunlight, ready to be picked and enjoyed.

Wild herbs and plants were also collected for their medicinal properties. The Cherokee used plants like ginseng, goldenseal, and yarrow to treat various ailments. This knowledge of herbal medicine was a vital part of their healthcare practices. Imagine an elder teaching a young apprentice how to identify and harvest medicinal plants, explaining their uses and the importance of respecting nature's gifts.

The Cherokee's hunting, fishing, and gathering practices were not just about survival; they were deeply connected to their spiritual beliefs and cultural traditions. They believed that all living things had spirits and that these spirits should be honored and respected. Ceremonies and rituals were performed to give thanks for the animals and plants that provided sustenance.

One such ritual was the hunting ceremony, performed before a hunt to ask for success and to show respect for the animals. Imagine the hunters gathered in a circle, offering prayers and songs to the spirits, seeking their blessings for a successful hunt. This ceremony reinforced the connection between the Cherokee and the natural world, reminding them of their responsibilities as stewards of the land.

traditional cherokee clothing and how it was made

The primary material for traditional Cherokee clothing was deerskin. Deer were abundant in the Cherokee homeland, and their hides provided a durable and flexible material for clothing. Picture a Cherokee hunter returning from a successful hunt, carrying the deer that would provide food, tools, and hides for the village. Once the meat was prepared and preserved, the hide was carefully treated to make it suitable for clothing.

The process of preparing deerskin was labor-intensive and required great skill. First, the hide was scraped clean of any remaining flesh and hair. This was done using sharp stones or bone tools. Imagine a group of women working together, their hands moving rhythmically as they scrape the hides, preparing them for tanning. The next step was to soften the hide, which involved soaking it in water and then stretching it repeatedly to make it pliable.

To further soften the hide and make it more durable, the Cherokee used a tanning process involving natural materials. They would often use the brains of the deer, which contain enzymes that help to break down tough fibers. The hide was soaked in a mixture of water and deer brains, then stretched and worked until it became soft and supple. Imagine the transformation of the hide, from a raw, stiff material to a soft, flexible piece of leather ready to be made into clothing.

Once the deerskin was prepared, it could be cut and sewn into various garments. Men typically wore breechcloths, leggings, and moccasins. The breechcloth was a simple piece of deerskin worn around the waist and passed between the legs, secured by a belt. Leggings, also made from deerskin, were tied to the belt and covered the legs, providing protection from the elements and rough terrain. Moccasins were soft, comfortable shoes made from a single piece of deerskin, stitched together with sinew or plant fibers. Picture a Cherokee man dressed in his traditional attire, ready for a day of hunting or traveling through the forest.

Women's clothing was also made from deerskin, but their garments were often more elaborate. They wore wraparound skirts, tunics, and mantles, decorated with intricate beadwork and fringe. The skirts were made from a single piece of deerskin, wrapped around the waist and fastened with a belt. The tunics were simple, loose-fitting garments that provided comfort and ease of movement. Mantles, or shawls, were draped over the shoulders for added warmth and decoration. Imagine a Cherokee woman dressed in her beautifully adorned clothing, each piece reflecting her skill and creativity.

The decoration of clothing was an important aspect of Cherokee culture. Beadwork, made from shells, stones, and later, glass beads obtained through trade, was used to create intricate patterns and designs. The beads were sewn onto the deerskin using sinew or plant fibers, forming geometric shapes, animals, and symbols that held cultural significance. Imagine the careful hands of a Cherokee woman as she stitches each bead into place, creating a work of art that tells a story of her heritage and identity.

In addition to beadwork, fringe was a common decorative element. Fringe was made by cutting the edges of the deerskin into long, narrow strips, which would then be left to hang freely. This not only added a decorative touch but also helped to channel rainwater away from the body, keeping the wearer dry. Picture the movement of the fringe as a Cherokee person walks or dances, the strips swaying and adding a dynamic element to the clothing.

During colder months, the Cherokee would wear cloaks or mantles made from animal fur, such as rabbit or bear. These fur garments provided much-needed warmth and were often worn over deerskin clothing. Imagine the cozy feel of a fur cloak wrapped around you on a chilly winter day, the soft fur providing insulation against the cold.

Accessories were also an important part of traditional Cherokee attire. Men and women both wore belts, sashes, and headbands, often decorated with beadwork and other embellishments. Belts and sashes were used to secure clothing and add a decorative element, while headbands were worn to keep hair out of the face and add a touch of style. Picture a Cherokee warrior with a beaded headband, ready for battle or a ceremonial dance, his attire reflecting his status and role within the community.

For special occasions and ceremonies, the Cherokee wore even more elaborate clothing. Ceremonial attire often featured additional decorations, such as feathers, painted designs, and more extensive beadwork. These garments were worn during important events, such as the Green Corn Ceremony, which celebrated the harvest and renewal of life. Imagine the vibrant colors and intricate designs of ceremonial clothing, each piece carefully crafted to honor the significance of the occasion.

Hair styles also played a role in traditional Cherokee appearance. Men often shaved their heads except for a single lock of hair, which was sometimes decorated with feathers or beads. This hairstyle, known as a scalp lock, was both practical and symbolic. Women typically wore their hair long, either loose or in braids, often adorned with beads and other decorations. Picture the careful grooming and decoration of hair, an important aspect of personal presentation and cultural identity.

importance of beadwork, pottery, and basket weaving

Beadwork was a highly valued skill among the Cherokee, with beads used to decorate clothing, accessories, and ceremonial items. Each bead was a tiny piece of a larger pattern, carefully chosen and placed to create beautiful, intricate designs.

Imagine the careful hands of a Cherokee artisan, threading each bead onto a sinew thread, creating patterns that might represent animals, plants, or abstract shapes. The beads were made from various materials, including shells, stones, and later, glass obtained through trade.

Beadwork was not only a form of artistic expression but also a way to convey stories and cultural symbols. Each design had its own meaning, telling stories of the Cherokee people, their beliefs, and their environment. Picture a young Cherokee girl learning beadwork from her mother or grandmother, sitting together as they create a beaded belt or moccasins, sharing stories and passing down traditions. This practice strengthened family bonds and ensured that cultural knowledge was preserved and shared across generations.

Pottery was another essential craft in Cherokee culture. The Cherokee made pottery for both everyday use and special occasions, creating bowls, pots, and other containers from the clay found in their homeland. The process of making pottery involved several steps, each requiring skill and patience. Imagine a Cherokee woman gathering clay from a riverbank, feeling the cool, sticky earth in her hands as she prepares to create a new piece.

The clay was first cleaned and then mixed with water to create a workable consistency. The potter would then shape the clay using a technique called coiling, where long ropes of clay were stacked and smoothed to form the desired shape. Picture the potter's hands moving gracefully, shaping and smoothing the clay, turning it into a beautiful and functional object. Once the piece was shaped, it was left to dry before being fired in an open pit or a specially constructed kiln.

Cherokee pottery was often decorated with intricate designs, either incised into the clay or painted on before firing. These decorations were not just for aesthetic purposes; they held cultural significance and reflected the artist's connection to their heritage. Imagine a pot adorned with patterns that represent the flowing rivers, the lush forests, or the animals that roamed the Cherokee homeland. Each piece of pottery was unique, a testament to the artist's skill and creativity.

Basket weaving was another crucial craft for the Cherokee, with baskets used for a wide range of purposes, from carrying food and supplies to storing items and even for ceremonial use. Baskets were made from natural materials such as river cane, white oak, and hickory bark, which were harvested and prepared with care. Imagine a Cherokee family heading into the forest to gather materials, selecting the best canes and bark for their baskets.

The process of basket weaving began with splitting the cane or bark into thin strips, which were then soaked in water to make them flexible. The weaver would then start the basket by creating a base and gradually building up the sides using various weaving techniques. Picture the weaver's hands moving deftly, interlacing the strips in a precise pattern, creating a sturdy and beautiful basket. The process required patience and skill, as each strip needed to be placed correctly to ensure the basket's strength and durability.

Like beadwork and pottery, basket weaving was an art form that was passed down through generations. Young girls and boys would learn the craft from their parents and grandparents, practicing the techniques and learning the patterns that had been used for centuries. This not only ensured the survival of the craft but also fostered a sense of continuity and connection to the past.

The importance of these crafts extended beyond their practical uses. Beadwork, pottery, and basket weaving were integral to Cherokee social and ceremonial life. Baskets were used in important ceremonies and rituals, such as the Green Corn Ceremony, where they held sacred items and offerings. Pottery was used to prepare and serve food during communal feasts and celebrations. Beaded items were worn during dances and ceremonies, adding to the beauty and significance of these events.

These crafts also played a role in trade and interaction with other tribes and European settlers. Cherokee beadwork, pottery, and baskets were highly prized for their quality and beauty, making them valuable trade items. This exchange of goods helped to establish and maintain relationships with neighboring tribes and settlers, facilitating the flow of ideas and cultural practices.

As we explore the importance of beadwork, pottery, and basket weaving in Cherokee culture, we see how these crafts were more than just ways to create objects. They were expressions of identity, culture, and community, woven into the fabric of daily life and special occasions. Each bead, pot, and basket told a story, reflecting the skills, values, and traditions of the Cherokee people.

3 / culture and traditions

introduction to the cherokee language

THE CHEROKEE LANGUAGE, known as Tsalagi, is part of the Iroquoian language family. It is unique and distinct, with its own sounds, grammar, and vocabulary. The language is deeply intertwined with the Cherokee way of life, reflecting their environment, beliefs, and social structure. Imagine a conversation between two Cherokee people, each word carefully chosen and filled with meaning, connecting them not just to each other but to their history and culture.

One of the most remarkable aspects of the Cherokee language is its writing system, developed by a Cherokee man named Sequoyah in the early 19th century. Sequoyah saw the need for a written form of the language to preserve and transmit Cherokee knowledge and culture. He created a syllabary, a set of written symbols that represent syllables rather than individual sounds. This was a revolutionary development, making it much easier to learn to read and write in Cherokee.

Picture Sequoyah working tirelessly, testing and refining his syllabary, driven by his vision of a literate Cherokee people. The syllabary consists of 85 symbols, each representing a unique syllable in the Cherokee language. This innovation allowed the Cherokee people to write their own stories, laws, and correspondence, preserving their language and culture for future generations. Imagine the excitement and pride of the Cherokee community when they first saw their language written down, their voices captured in a way that would endure.

Learning the Cherokee syllabary can be a fun and engaging activity. Each symbol has a distinct shape, and practicing writing them is like learning a secret code. Imagine sitting down with a piece of paper and a pencil, carefully drawing each symbol, and then sounding out the syllables they represent. You might start with simple words like "ᎵᏍᏝ" (di-ga-da) meaning "corn" or "ᎤᏃᎩ" (ka-no-gi) meaning "turkey," gradually building your vocabulary as you become more familiar with the symbols.

The Cherokee language is rich in vocabulary that reflects the natural world and the Cherokee way of life. For example, there are specific words for different types of trees, animals, and plants found in the Appalachian region. This precise vocabulary shows the deep connection the Cherokee have with their environment. Imagine learning the Cherokee words for the things you see every day in nature, like "ᏧᏍᏆᎦ" (tsu-s-qua-ga) for "bird" or "ᎩᏟ" (gi-tli) for "dog." Each word is a piece of the larger puzzle of the Cherokee world.

The grammar of the Cherokee language is also fascinating. Unlike English, which often relies on word order to convey meaning, Cherokee uses a complex system of prefixes, suffixes, and infixes to modify words. This means that a single Cherokee word can contain a lot of information. For example, the word "ᏩᏙ" (wa-do) means "thank you," but it can be modified to express different levels of politeness or specificity. Imagine learning how to build words in Cherokee, each part adding a new layer of meaning and nuance.

Listening to the Cherokee language spoken aloud is like listening to music. The rhythm and intonation of the language give it a melodic quality. Imagine sitting around a fire, listening to an elder tell a story in Cherokee, the words flowing in a way that captivates and transports you. The stories told in Cherokee carry the wisdom and traditions of the Cherokee people, passed down through generations.

One of the challenges facing the Cherokee language today is the need for revitalization. Like many Indigenous languages, Cherokee has seen a decline in the number of fluent speakers. However, there are many efforts underway to keep the language alive. Cherokee schools teach the language to young students, ensuring that the next generation can speak, read, and write in Cherokee. Community programs and online resources also provide opportunities for people of all ages to learn and practice the language. Imagine being part of a language class, learning alongside others who share a passion for keeping the Cherokee language vibrant and strong.

Technology has also played a role in the revitalization of the Cherokee language. Apps, websites, and social media platforms offer new ways to learn and use the language. Imagine playing a game on your tablet that helps you practice Cherokee vocabulary or using a language app to chat with friends in Cherokee. These modern tools make learning the language accessible and fun, bringing it into everyday life.

The Cherokee language is more than just a way to communicate; it is a living expression of the Cherokee identity. Each word, phrase, and story carries with it the history, values, and spirit of the Cherokee people. By learning and using the Cherokee language, we honor and preserve this rich cultural heritage, ensuring that it continues to thrive for generations to come.

importance of storytelling

Storytelling holds a special place in Cherokee life because it serves multiple purposes. It is a tool for education, a method for preserving history, and a way to instill values and morals.

Sarah Michaels

Through stories, the Cherokee people learned about their ancestors, their beliefs, and the natural world around them. Imagine listening to a tale about why the possum has a bare tail or how the first fire was brought to the people. These stories are rich with lessons and insights, cleverly woven into engaging narratives.

One of the most important aspects of storytelling is its role in education. Cherokee stories often contain lessons about life, nature, and human behavior. For example, a story might teach the importance of cooperation, bravery, or respect for the environment. These lessons are wrapped in engaging tales that captivate listeners, making the learning process enjoyable and memorable. Imagine a young Cherokee boy listening to the story of "The Rabbit and the Tar Wolf," learning about the consequences of trickery and the value of cleverness and quick thinking.

"The Rabbit and the Tar Wolf" is one such popular Cherokee legend. In this story, Rabbit is a trickster known for his cleverness. However, one day he meets his match in the Tar Wolf, a figure made from sticky tar and set as a trap by his enemies. Rabbit, thinking the Tar Wolf is a real animal, gets stuck when he tries to fight it. This story teaches about the dangers of underestimating others and the pitfalls of overconfidence. Imagine the laughter and gasps of the children as the elder narrates Rabbit's predicament, each twist and turn of the story reinforcing the lesson.

Another beloved legend is the story of how the first fire came to the Cherokee people. According to the legend, the animals lived in a time of darkness and cold. The only fire was kept by the Thunder Beings, high up in the mountains. The animals held a council to decide who would go and bring back the fire. Many tried and failed, but it was the humble Water Spider who succeeded. She wove a tiny bowl of web, carried an ember back, and shared it with all the animals, bringing warmth and light to the world. This story highlights themes of bravery, humility, and the importance of even the smallest creatures. Picture the children's eyes lighting up as they hear about the brave little Water Spider, understanding that everyone has a valuable role to play.

Storytelling also helps preserve the history and traditions of the Cherokee people. Before the creation of the Cherokee syllabary, stories were the primary way to pass down knowledge. Elders would recount tales of great leaders, significant events, and ancestral traditions. These stories kept the past alive and ensured that the community remembered where they came from. Imagine an elder recounting the story of Sequoyah and the creation of the Cherokee syllabary, inspiring pride and respect for their written language and its importance in preserving their culture.

One such historical legend is the story of Tsali, a Cherokee hero who resisted removal during the Trail of Tears. Tsali and his family fled into the mountains to avoid being forcibly relocated. They were eventually captured, but Tsali's sacrifice allowed some Cherokee people to remain in their homeland. This story is a powerful reminder of the resilience and bravery of the Cherokee people. Imagine the solemn atmosphere as an elder tells this story, the listeners feeling a deep connection to their history and the sacrifices made by their ancestors.

Cherokee legends often include explanations for natural phenomena, providing a way to understand and relate to the world. For example, the story of "How the Milky Way Came to Be" explains the origin of the Milky Way. According to the legend, long ago, a great dog stole cornmeal from the people and ran across the sky, spilling the meal as he went. The spilled cornmeal formed the Milky Way, a band of stars that stretches across the night sky. This story not only explains a natural phenomenon but also reinforces the cultural significance of corn to the Cherokee people. Imagine gazing up at the stars, remembering the tale of the great dog, and feeling a sense of wonder and connection to the universe.

Another important aspect of storytelling is its role in bringing the community together. Stories were often told during gatherings and ceremonies, creating a sense of unity and shared experience. The act of listening to a story together helped to strengthen the bonds within the community. Imagine a cold winter night, families huddled together in their homes, sharing stories to pass the time and keep spirits high. These moments of togetherness were crucial for maintaining social cohesion and reinforcing communal values.

Cherokee storytelling also emphasizes the relationship between humans and nature. Many legends feature animals, plants, and natural forces as central characters, highlighting the interconnectedness of all living things. These stories teach respect for the environment and the importance of living in harmony with nature. For example, the story of "The Origin of Strawberries" tells how the first strawberries grew from the ground to bring a couple back together after an argument. This tale underscores the themes of love, forgiveness, and the beauty of nature. Imagine the sweetness of fresh strawberries and the deeper appreciation of their significance after hearing this story.

traditional cherokee music and instruments

The heartbeat of Cherokee music is the drum. Drums are considered sacred and are used in many ceremonies and dances. The steady, rhythmic beat of the drum is thought to mimic the heartbeat of the earth, connecting the people to the natural world. Imagine a circle of dancers moving in unison to the beat of a large drum, their feet pounding the earth in rhythm, creating a powerful and unified sound. The drumbeat is both grounding and uplifting, a pulse that binds the community together.

Cherokee drums come in various sizes and types. The most common are the water drum and the log drum. The water drum is made by stretching a hide over a small wooden frame or pot partially filled with water, which helps to create a resonant sound. Imagine the deep, echoing tones of the water drum, its sound carrying across the village and drawing people together. The log drum, on the other hand, is made from a hollowed-out log with openings cut into it. The drummer strikes the log with sticks, producing a distinctive, rhythmic beat. Picture the resonant, hollow sounds of the log drum, a beat that can be heard for miles, calling people to gather.

Flutes are another important instrument in Cherokee music. Made from river cane, wood, or bone, the flute produces a soft, melodic sound that is both soothing and evocative. Each flute is unique, often decorated with carvings and designs that reflect the maker's personality and the purpose of the instrument. Imagine sitting by a river, listening to the gentle notes of a flute mingling with the sounds of flowing water and singing birds. The music of the flute is often used in personal expression, storytelling, and courtship, its haunting melodies conveying deep emotions and stories.

Rattles are also essential to Cherokee music, adding texture and rhythm to songs and dances. Made from turtle shells, gourds, or carved wood, rattles are filled with small objects like pebbles or seeds that create sound when shaken. Imagine the lively sound of rattles, adding a crisp, rhythmic layer to the music, enhancing the overall experience. Rattles are often used in ceremonial dances, where their sound helps to keep the rhythm and add to the festive atmosphere.

The Cherokee also use other instruments like whistles, panpipes, and stringed instruments. Whistles, made from bone or wood, produce high-pitched, clear tones that can be used in both music and communication. Panpipes, made from a series of cane tubes of varying lengths, create a harmonic sound when blown across. Stringed instruments, like the Cherokee fiddle, are made from natural materials and add a rich, melodic dimension to their music. Imagine the harmonious blend of these instruments, each contributing its unique sound to create a rich tapestry of music.

Songs in Cherokee culture are passed down through generations, preserving history, traditions, and lessons. These songs often tell stories, celebrate important events, or convey spiritual messages. Imagine a group of elders singing a traditional song, their voices rising and falling in harmony, each note carrying the weight of centuries of tradition. The lyrics of these songs are rich with imagery and meaning, often reflecting the natural world and the values of the Cherokee people.

One important type of song is the Stomp Dance song. The Stomp Dance is a traditional Cherokee dance that involves a group of dancers moving in a counterclockwise circle around a fire. The dancers' movements are accompanied by the rhythm of turtle shell rattles worn on the legs of female dancers, creating a distinctive sound. Imagine the rhythmic stomping and the jingling of rattles, accompanied by the deep beat of the drum and the chanting of the singers. The Stomp Dance is both a social and a spiritual activity, reinforcing community bonds and connecting the dancers with the earth and the spirits.

Another significant song type is the Cherokee lullaby. These gentle, soothing songs are sung to infants and young children, helping them to sleep and conveying love and protection. Imagine a mother or grandmother rocking a baby, softly singing a lullaby in Cherokee, the tender words and melody creating a sense of peace and security. Lullabies are a beautiful example of how music is woven into the fabric of daily life, nurturing the next generation and passing on cultural traditions.

Cherokee music also includes ceremonial songs, used in various rituals and spiritual practices. These songs are often repetitive and rhythmic, designed to induce a meditative state or to invoke the presence of the spirits. Imagine a sacred ceremony, the air filled with the sound of drums, rattles, and chanting, each beat and note a call to the spiritual world. These ceremonial songs play a crucial role in maintaining the spiritual health and harmony of the community.

Music education is an essential part of Cherokee culture,

with children learning traditional songs and instruments from a young age. Elders and experienced musicians teach the younger generation, ensuring that the musical traditions are preserved and continued. Imagine a group of children gathered around an elder, learning to play the flute or drum, their small hands mimicking the movements of their teacher. Through this process, children not only learn the technical skills needed to make music but also gain a deeper understanding of their cultural heritage and values.

The role of music in Cherokee culture extends beyond entertainment; it is a vital means of communication and expression. Music is used to convey emotions, tell stories, and connect with both the community and the spiritual world. It is a powerful tool for preserving history and traditions, a means of educating and uniting the community, and a source of joy and inspiration.

types of dances and their significance

One of the most important and well-known Cherokee dances is the Stomp Dance. This dance is both a social and ceremonial event, typically performed at night around a central fire. The dance involves a leader, who begins the chant, followed by the dancers who respond in kind. The participants form a circle and move in a counterclockwise direction, their feet striking the ground in a rhythmic stomp. Imagine the rhythmic sound of feet hitting the earth, accompanied by the jingling of turtle shell rattles worn by the women on their legs. The Stomp Dance symbolizes unity and harmony with nature, as the dancers move together in sync with the heartbeat of the drum.

The Stomp Dance is more than just a dance; it is a way to connect with the earth and the spiritual world. The circular motion of the dance represents the cycle of life, the changing seasons, and the interconnectedness of all living things. Picture the flickering flames of the central fire casting shadows on the dancers, creating a mesmerizing scene that draws everyone into the shared experience. The chants and songs that accompany the dance often tell stories of creation, important events, and lessons from the past, reinforcing the cultural and spiritual teachings of the Cherokee.

Another significant dance is the Corn Dance, performed to celebrate the planting and harvesting of corn, a staple crop for the Cherokee people. The Corn Dance is a joyful and vibrant celebration, marked by gratitude and hope for a bountiful harvest. Imagine the village coming together in the spring to plant corn, everyone participating in the ceremony to ensure a successful growing season. The dance involves lively movements, singing, and drumming, creating an atmosphere of celebration and community spirit.

During the Corn Dance, participants may wear special clothing adorned with symbols of growth and fertility, such as corn husks and green leaves. The dance steps mimic the planting and growing process, with movements that resemble the sowing of seeds and the nurturing of young plants. Picture the dancers moving gracefully, their steps symbolizing the careful attention given to the crops, their songs expressing hope and gratitude for the abundance provided by the earth.

The Friendship Dance is another cherished Cherokee tradition, emphasizing the importance of unity and community. This dance is often performed at social gatherings, bringing people together to celebrate friendship and mutual support. Imagine a large circle of people, holding hands and moving together in a joyful, rhythmic pattern. The Friendship Dance is an inclusive event, where everyone, young and old, can participate, reinforcing the bonds within the community.

The steps of the Friendship Dance are simple and easy to follow, allowing everyone to join in and enjoy the experience. The dance often involves a series of movements that symbolize the act of coming together, such as crossing arms and weaving in and out of the circle. Picture the smiles and laughter of the dancers as they move together, the simple act of dancing creating a sense of connection and belonging.

The Eagle Dance is a ceremonial dance that holds great spiritual significance. It is performed to honor the eagle, a sacred bird in Cherokee culture that represents strength, courage, and connection to the Creator. The Eagle Dance is a way to seek guidance and blessings from the eagle spirit, asking for protection and insight. Imagine the dancers donning eagle feathers and moving with grace and power, their arms extended to mimic the wings of an eagle.

The movements of the Eagle Dance are designed to reflect the flight and behavior of the eagle. The dancers soar, dip, and glide, creating a visual representation of the eagle's journey through the sky. The dance is often accompanied by chants and drumming, creating a powerful and evocative atmosphere. Picture the dancers embodying the spirit of the eagle, their movements filled with reverence and respect for this majestic bird.

The Bear Dance is another significant ceremonial dance, performed to honor the bear, an important animal in Cherokee culture symbolizing strength, healing, and protection. The Bear Dance is often performed during the winter, a time when bears hibernate and the earth rests. The dance seeks to honor the bear's strength and to invoke its protective spirit for the community. Imagine the dancers wearing bear pelts and moving in a slow, deliberate manner, their steps heavy and powerful, mirroring the movements of a bear.

The Bear Dance involves deep, rhythmic drumming and low chants that create a grounding and powerful atmosphere. The dancers move in a circular pattern, their steps resonating with the beat of the drum, invoking the presence and power of the bear spirit. Picture the intense focus and dedication of the dancers, each movement a tribute to the strength and resilience of the bear.

The Snake Dance is another unique and important dance, performed to ensure harmony and balance in the community. The dance involves intricate, serpentine movements, with dancers weaving in and out of a long line, mimicking the movement of a snake. The Snake Dance symbolizes the importance of adaptability and the need to navigate the challenges of life with grace and flexibility. Imagine the dancers moving smoothly and fluidly, their bodies undulating like a snake, creating a mesmerizing and continuous flow of motion.

The dance is often accompanied by rattles and drums, adding to the rhythmic and hypnotic quality of the performance. The Snake Dance teaches valuable lessons about the need for balance and harmony, both within oneself and within the community. Picture the audience watching in awe as the dancers move seamlessly, each step reinforcing the importance of unity and cooperation.

major cherokee festivals and their meanings

One of the most significant Cherokee festivals is the Green Corn Ceremony, also known as the Busk. This festival takes place in late summer when the corn is ready to harvest. It is a time of thanksgiving, renewal, and purification. Picture the village coming alive with preparations, everyone involved in cleaning and decorating their homes, and preparing food for the feast. The Green Corn Ceremony is a multi-day event that includes fasting, dancing, and various rituals to cleanse the body and spirit.

The festival begins with a period of fasting and prayer, where the Cherokee people reflect on the past year and seek to purify themselves. Imagine the quiet, introspective atmosphere as people meditate and prepare for the days ahead. The community then gathers at the central plaza, where a new fire is kindled to symbolize the start of a new cycle. The fire is a sacred element, representing the renewal of life and the connection to the Great Spirit. Picture the flames rising in the night, casting a warm glow on the faces of the participants, as the new fire is lit and blessed.

The Green Corn Ceremony also includes a series of dances and songs, each with its own meaning and purpose. One of the central dances is the Stomp Dance, performed around the new fire. The dancers move in a counterclockwise circle, their feet striking the ground in rhythm with the beat of the drum and the jingling of turtle shell rattles. Imagine the powerful, rhythmic sound filling the air, the dancers moving in unison, their movements symbolizing the harmony and unity of the community.

Another important festival is the Great New Moon Ceremony, which marks the beginning of the new year according to the Cherokee lunar calendar. This festival usually takes place in October or November, coinciding with the appearance of the new moon. The Great New Moon Ceremony is a time to celebrate the end of the harvest and to prepare for the coming winter. Imagine the village illuminated by the light of the new moon, everyone gathering to welcome the new year with joy and anticipation.

The ceremony involves lighting a sacred fire, which is kept burning throughout the festival. The fire represents the sun and its life-giving energy, a reminder of the eternal cycle of life and the importance of renewal. Picture the villagers gathered around the fire, offering prayers and blessings for the new year, asking for protection and prosperity. The festival includes feasting, dancing, and storytelling, creating a festive and communal atmosphere.

During the Great New Moon Ceremony, special dances are performed to honor the spirits and to ensure a good start to the new year. One of these dances is the Eagle Dance, which pays tribute to the eagle, a symbol of strength, courage, and connection to the Creator. Imagine the dancers adorned with eagle feathers, moving gracefully and powerfully, their arms extended like wings, mimicking the flight of the eagle. The dance is accompanied by drumming and chanting, creating a powerful and uplifting experience.

The Cherokee also celebrate the First New Moon of Spring, another important festival that marks the beginning of the planting season. This festival usually takes place in March or

April, when the first new moon appears after the spring equinox. The First New Moon of Spring is a time to honor the earth and to ask for blessings for the new crops. Imagine the fresh, spring air filled with the sounds of birds and the scent of blooming flowers, as the community gathers to welcome the new season.

During this festival, the Cherokee perform the Planting Dance, a ritual that involves dancing and singing to encourage the growth of the crops. The dancers move in a circular pattern, mimicking the sowing of seeds and the nurturing of young plants. Picture the vibrant, colorful clothing of the dancers, decorated with symbols of growth and fertility, as they move gracefully and rhythmically. The Planting Dance is a way to connect with the earth and to express gratitude for the abundance it provides.

The Cherokee also celebrate the Ripe Corn Ceremony, which takes place in late summer when the corn is fully mature. This festival is a time to give thanks for the harvest and to share the abundance with the community. Imagine the village filled with the golden glow of ripe corn, the air thick with the scent of roasting ears, and the sounds of laughter and joy. The Ripe Corn Ceremony is marked by feasting, dancing, and communal activities, reinforcing the bonds within the community.

During the Ripe Corn Ceremony, special rituals are performed to honor the spirits of the corn and to ensure a good harvest in the future. One such ritual is the Corn Blessing, where the first ears of corn are offered to the Great Spirit as a sign of gratitude. Picture the solemn, reverent atmosphere as the corn is blessed and offered, the community gathered in silence and reflection. The festival also includes the Corn Dance, a joyful celebration of the harvest, with dancers moving in a lively and energetic pattern, their movements expressing the gratitude and joy of the community.

Another significant festival is the Cherokee New Fire Ceremony, which takes place in late winter or early spring. This festival is a time to cleanse and renew the community, both physically and spiritually. Imagine the village preparing for the New Fire Ceremony, everyone involved in cleaning their homes and preparing for the new fire. The ceremony begins with extinguishing all the old fires in the village, symbolizing the end of the old year and the beginning of a new one.

A new fire is then kindled using a traditional fire-starting method, often by rubbing sticks together to create sparks. Picture the excitement and anticipation as the first sparks fly and the new fire is lit, its flames rising high and bright. The new fire is a symbol of renewal and purification, a reminder of the eternal cycle of life and the importance of starting fresh. The New Fire Ceremony includes various rituals, dances, and songs, each with its own significance and purpose.

how these festivals are celebrated

As the sun rises, the village awakens to the sounds of children laughing and adults calling out to each other, setting the tone for a day filled with excitement. The first task of the day might be cleaning and purifying the living spaces. Families work together, sweeping the floors, washing the walls, and tidying up their homes. This act of cleaning is symbolic, representing the removal of negative energy and making way for new, positive beginnings. Imagine the sense of satisfaction and anticipation as the villagers prepare their homes for the festivities ahead.

In preparation for the Green Corn Ceremony, for example, the entire community participates in gathering and preparing the new harvest. Corn is husked, beans are sorted, and squash is harvested. Picture the village square filled with baskets of fresh produce, the air thick with the aroma of roasting corn. The central plaza is decorated with green corn stalks and other symbols of fertility and growth, creating a vibrant and festive atmosphere.

The ceremony begins with a period of fasting and prayer, a

time for individuals to reflect and purify their bodies and spirits. Imagine the quiet, contemplative moments as people gather in small groups or sit alone, meditating and offering prayers. This spiritual preparation sets the stage for the communal events to follow, fostering a sense of inner peace and readiness.

As the fast comes to an end, the new fire is kindled. This sacred act involves lighting a fire using traditional methods, often by rubbing sticks together to create sparks. The new fire symbolizes renewal and the start of a new cycle. Picture the community gathered around, watching intently as the first sparks fly and the flames take hold. The fire is then blessed by the elders, who offer prayers and songs to honor its significance.

With the new fire burning brightly, the celebrations move into the realm of music and dance. The Stomp Dance is a central part of the Green Corn Ceremony, bringing everyone together in a powerful, rhythmic expression of unity. Participants form a circle around the fire, moving in a counterclockwise direction. The beat of the drum sets the pace, while the jingling of turtle shell rattles adds a lively, percussive element. Imagine the synchronized movements of the dancers, their feet striking the ground in unison, creating a palpable energy that resonates throughout the village.

The dancers are led by a song leader, who begins the chant, followed by the rest of the group. The call-and-response pattern of the songs adds to the communal spirit, with each voice contributing to the overall harmony. Picture the faces of the dancers, illuminated by the firelight, as they sing and move together, their expressions reflecting the joy and reverence of the moment.

Feasting is another integral part of festival celebrations. For the Green Corn Ceremony, a communal meal is prepared using the newly harvested crops. Long tables are set up in the central plaza, laden with dishes made from corn, beans, squash, and other seasonal foods. Imagine the delicious smells wafting through the air as pots of stew simmer and cornbread bakes. The community gathers to share this meal, giving thanks for the abundance provided by the earth.

During the Great New Moon Ceremony, the focus shifts to celebrating the end of the harvest and the beginning of the new year. The festival starts with the lighting of a sacred fire, similar to the Green Corn Ceremony. This fire is kept burning throughout the festival, serving as a constant reminder of the sun's life-giving energy. Imagine the villagers gathered around the fire, offering prayers and blessings for the new year, their faces aglow with hope and anticipation.

Special dances are performed to honor the spirits and to ensure a good start to the new year. The Eagle Dance, for example, is a highlight of the Great New Moon Ceremony. Dancers wear eagle feathers and move with grace and power, mimicking the flight of the eagle. The dance is accompanied by drumming and chanting, creating a powerful and uplifting atmosphere. Picture the dancers, their arms extended like wings, soaring and gliding in a beautiful, symbolic representation of the eagle's journey.

The First New Moon of Spring marks the beginning of the planting season and is celebrated with the Planting Dance. This dance involves movements that mimic the sowing of seeds and the nurturing of young plants. Participants dress in vibrant clothing adorned with symbols of growth and fertility, adding to the festive atmosphere. Imagine the dancers moving gracefully, their steps reflecting the careful attention given to the crops, their songs expressing gratitude and hope for a successful growing season.

The Ripe Corn Ceremony, celebrated in late summer, is a joyful time to give thanks for the harvest. The festival is marked by feasting, dancing, and communal activities. Corn, being the central element, is prepared in various ways – roasted, boiled, and made into bread. Imagine the village filled with the golden glow of ripe corn, the air thick with the scent of roasting ears, and the sounds of laughter and joy as people gather to celebrate the bounty of the harvest.

The New Fire Ceremony, celebrated in late winter or early spring, focuses on cleansing and renewal. The festival begins with extinguishing all old fires in the village, symbolizing the end of the old year. A new fire is then kindled using traditional fire-starting methods. This act of renewal is followed by various rituals, dances, and songs, each with its own significance. Picture the community coming together, watching as the first sparks fly and the new fire takes hold, its flames rising high and bright.

Throughout these festivals, storytelling plays a crucial role. Elders recount tales of creation, important events, and lessons from the past, reinforcing cultural and spiritual teachings. Imagine the village gathering around a fire in the evening, listening intently to the stories, their imaginations captivated by the rich imagery and wisdom contained in the tales.

Music, too, is a vital part of the celebrations. Drumming, flutes, and rattles create a lively and festive atmosphere, adding to the joy and excitement of the festivals. Imagine the rhythmic beats of the drums, the melodic sounds of the flutes, and the lively jingling of the rattles filling the air, creating a vibrant soundscape that resonates throughout the village.

4 / governance and society

structure of cherokee leadership and councils

LEADERSHIP IN A CHEROKEE village is typically divided between two main roles: the Peace Chief and the War Chief. These leaders guide the community in times of peace and conflict, respectively, and work together to maintain balance and harmony. Picture the Peace Chief, often an elder known for wisdom and diplomacy, leading the village in making decisions about daily life, ceremonial practices, and internal disputes. The Peace Chief is a figure of stability and guidance, embodying the values of peace and harmony.

The War Chief, on the other hand, is responsible for the defense and protection of the community. This role requires bravery, strategic thinking, and the ability to lead in times of conflict. Imagine the War Chief preparing the warriors for a hunt or organizing the defense of the village against external threats. The War Chief is respected for their courage and leadership in ensuring the safety and security of the people.

Central to Cherokee governance is the council, a group of representatives from each clan who come together to discuss and make decisions on behalf of the village. The council operates on a system of consensus, meaning that decisions are made only when all members agree. This process can be lengthy, but it ensures that everyone's voice is heard and that decisions reflect the collective will of the community. Picture a council meeting, where representatives sit in a circle, discussing issues and working together to find solutions. The atmosphere is one of respect and cooperation, with each person contributing their perspective.

The council is typically divided into two groups: the White Council and the Red Council. The White Council, led by the Peace Chief, deals with issues related to peace, agriculture, and social matters. They focus on maintaining harmony within the village, resolving disputes, and organizing communal activities. Imagine the White Council discussing plans for the upcoming Green Corn Ceremony, ensuring that all preparations are in place for a successful celebration.

The Red Council, led by the War Chief, handles matters related to war, hunting, and external relations. They are responsible for the village's defense and for making decisions about conflicts with other tribes or settlers. Picture the Red Council strategizing about a hunting expedition or discussing ways to protect the village from potential threats. The Red Council's decisions are crucial for the security and sustenance of the community.

Both councils work closely together, reflecting the Cherokee belief in balance and the interconnectedness of all aspects of life. While the Peace Chief and the War Chief have distinct roles, they collaborate to ensure the well-being of the village. This dual leadership system ensures that both peace and protection are prioritized, creating a stable and resilient community.

The Cherokee clan system also plays a vital role in governance. Each person belongs to one of seven clans: Wolf, Deer, Bird, Long Hair, Wild Potato, Blue, and Paint. Clan membership is matrilineal, meaning it is inherited through the mother's line. The clans are responsible for various social and ceremonial roles within the village. Imagine a village where each clan contributes its unique skills and knowledge, ensuring that all aspects of life are cared for and celebrated.

Clan leaders, or clan mothers, are respected figures who provide guidance and support to their clan members. These leaders play a crucial role in maintaining the social fabric of the community, resolving internal disputes, and representing their clan in council meetings. Picture a clan mother advising a young woman on her responsibilities within the clan or helping to mediate a disagreement between clan members. The wisdom and experience of the clan leaders are invaluable to the functioning of the village.

During council meetings, each clan is represented by its leader or a chosen spokesperson. This ensures that all clans have a voice in the decision-making process. The council meetings are often held in a central council house, a large, circular building designed to accommodate all representatives. Imagine the council house filled with the buzz of conversation, as representatives discuss issues, share ideas, and work towards consensus. The circular arrangement of seating reflects the equality and unity of the council members.

Decision-making in the council is a careful and deliberate process. Representatives listen to each other's viewpoints, consider the implications of their decisions, and strive to reach a consensus that benefits the entire community. This process emphasizes the importance of dialogue, patience, and mutual respect. Picture a representative standing to speak, carefully presenting their perspective, while others listen attentively, ready to discuss and consider the points raised.

In addition to the village council, the Cherokee also have a larger council that includes representatives from multiple villages. This regional council addresses broader issues that affect several communities, such as trade, alliances, and conflicts. Imagine representatives traveling from different villages to gather in a central location, bringing news and concerns from their communities, and working together to make decisions that impact the broader Cherokee nation.

The structure of Cherokee leadership and councils is a reflection of their cultural values: the emphasis on consensus, the balance between peace and protection, and the importance of community and clan. Through this system, the Cherokee ensure that their governance is inclusive, respectful, and effective in addressing the needs of their people.

role of chiefs and clan leaders

The Peace Chief and the War Chief are the primary leaders within the Cherokee governance system, each with distinct roles and responsibilities. The Peace Chief is often an elder chosen for their wisdom, experience, and ability to maintain harmony within the village. Imagine the Peace Chief sitting with community members, listening attentively to their concerns, and offering thoughtful advice. This role is about nurturing relationships, resolving conflicts, and ensuring that the village operates smoothly.

The Peace Chief oversees the White Council, which deals with matters related to peace, agriculture, and social issues. Picture the Peace Chief presiding over a council meeting, where representatives discuss plans for the upcoming Green Corn Ceremony or strategies for managing communal resources. The Peace Chief's guidance helps ensure that decisions reflect the collective will and promote the well-being of the entire community.

In contrast, the War Chief is responsible for the village's defense and protection. This role requires bravery, strategic thinking, and leadership during times of conflict. The War Chief leads the Red Council, which handles issues related to war, hunting, and external threats. Imagine the War Chief organizing a hunting party or strategizing ways to protect the village from potential dangers. The War Chief's role is crucial in safeguarding the community and ensuring that the people are prepared for any challenges they might face.

Both chiefs work closely together, balancing the needs for peace and protection. Their collaboration reflects the Cherokee belief in the interconnectedness of all aspects of life and the importance of maintaining harmony and balance. Picture the Peace Chief and War Chief consulting each other, combining their insights and expertise to make decisions that benefit the village as a whole. This dual leadership system ensures that both the spiritual and physical well-being of the community are prioritized.

Clan leaders, often referred to as clan mothers or clan elders, also play vital roles within Cherokee society. Each person belongs to one of seven clans: Wolf, Deer, Bird, Long Hair, Wild Potato, Blue, and Paint. These clans are matrilineal, meaning membership is inherited through the mother's line. The clan leaders provide guidance, support, and representation for their clan members, ensuring that the needs and concerns of each clan are addressed.

Imagine a clan mother, a respected elder who offers advice and support to her clan members. She might mediate disputes, provide guidance on personal and communal matters, and represent her clan in council meetings. Picture a young woman seeking advice from her clan mother, discussing her role within the clan and the responsibilities she carries. The clan mother's wisdom and experience are invaluable in helping her clan navigate the complexities of daily life and maintain their cultural traditions.

Clan leaders also play a crucial role in ceremonial and social activities. They help organize and lead rituals, ensuring that traditions are upheld and that the community remains connected to their cultural heritage. Imagine the clan leaders coordinating preparations for the Great New Moon Ceremony, ensuring that each aspect of the celebration reflects the values and beliefs of the Cherokee people. Their leadership helps create a sense of continuity and shared identity within the community.

During council meetings, clan leaders represent their clan's interests and contribute to the decision-making process. This ensures that all voices are heard and that decisions reflect the diverse perspectives within the village. Picture a council meeting where clan leaders discuss a proposal for a new agricultural project, each leader offering insights based on their clan's experiences and needs. The collaborative nature of these discussions helps build consensus and fosters a sense of unity and cooperation.

The role of chiefs and clan leaders extends beyond governance and decision-making; they are also custodians of Cherokee culture and values. Through their leadership, they model the principles of respect, harmony, and community service. Imagine a Peace Chief teaching young children about the importance of living in harmony with nature or a clan mother sharing stories of their ancestors, instilling a sense of pride and identity in the next generation. Their efforts help ensure that Cherokee traditions and values are passed down and preserved.

Leadership within the Cherokee community is not about exerting power or control; it is about serving the people and fostering a sense of collective responsibility. Chiefs and clan leaders are chosen based on their ability to guide, support, and inspire others. Their authority is rooted in respect and trust, earned through their actions and dedication to the well-being of the community. Picture a War Chief leading by example, demonstrating courage and integrity, and inspiring others to follow in their footsteps.

In times of crisis, the leadership of the chiefs and clan leaders is especially crucial. They provide stability, guidance, and reassurance, helping the community navigate challenges and emerge stronger. Imagine a village facing a difficult winter, with food supplies running low. The Peace Chief and War Chief, along with the clan leaders, work together to develop a plan to ensure that everyone has enough to eat and that the community remains united and resilient.

The role of chiefs and clan leaders is also essential in maintaining relationships with other tribes and external groups. They represent the community in diplomatic matters, forging alliances, and resolving conflicts. Picture the Peace Chief meeting with leaders from neighboring tribes to discuss mutual interests and build cooperative relationships. Their ability to navigate these external interactions helps protect and strengthen the community.

explanation of the cherokee clan system

The Cherokee people have seven clans: Wolf, Deer, Bird, Long Hair, Wild Potato, Blue, and Paint. Each clan has its own unique characteristics, roles, and responsibilities within the community. Membership in a clan is matrilineal, meaning it is inherited through the mother's line. This means that a child belongs to the same clan as their mother. Imagine a young boy proudly saying that he is part of the Wolf Clan, just like his mother and her mother before her.

The Wolf Clan is the largest and most prominent of the Cherokee clans. Members of the Wolf Clan are often associated with leadership and protection. Many of the Peace Chiefs and War Chiefs come from this clan. Picture a member of the Wolf Clan taking on the role of a protector, ensuring the safety and well-being of the village. The clan's strong and courageous characteristics make them natural leaders and guardians of the community.

The Deer Clan is known for its skills in hunting and outdoor activities. Members of the Deer Clan are often responsible for providing food for the community and are skilled in tracking and hunting game. Imagine a group of Deer Clan members heading into the forest on a hunting expedition, their knowledge of the land and animal behavior ensuring a successful hunt. Their role is vital for the sustenance of the village, and they are respected for their abilities and contributions.

The Bird Clan is associated with spirituality and communication with the spirit world. Members of the Bird Clan often serve as spiritual leaders and healers. They are believed to have a special connection with the divine and are responsible for leading ceremonies and rituals. Picture a Bird Clan member performing a healing ritual, their chants and prayers invoking the spirits to bring health and well-being to a sick community member. Their spiritual guidance helps maintain the balance and harmony of the village.

The Long Hair Clan is known for its emphasis on beauty, peace, and diplomacy. Members of this clan often serve as diplomats and negotiators, helping to resolve conflicts and build relationships with other tribes. Imagine a Long Hair Clan member visiting a neighboring village to discuss a treaty or resolve a dispute, their calm and diplomatic nature ensuring a peaceful outcome. The Long Hair Clan's focus on harmony and beauty also makes them skilled artisans and musicians, enriching the cultural life of the community.

The Wild Potato Clan, also known as the Bear Clan, is associated with agriculture and plant knowledge. Members of this clan are responsible for farming and gathering wild plants. They possess extensive knowledge of medicinal herbs and plants and often serve as herbalists and healers. Picture a Wild Potato Clan member tending to the fields, their expertise ensuring a bountiful harvest, or gathering herbs from the forest to create remedies for various ailments. Their connection to the land and plant life is essential for the health and well-being of the community.

The Blue Clan is associated with medicine and healing. Members of this clan are known for their knowledge of medicinal plants and traditional healing practices. They often serve as doctors and healers within the village. Imagine a Blue Clan member preparing a mixture of herbs to treat a sick child, their extensive knowledge and skill bringing relief and healing.

Their role is crucial in maintaining the health and vitality of the community.

The Paint Clan is known for its creativity and artistic abilities. Members of this clan are skilled in painting, crafting, and other forms of artistic expression. They often create the decorations and symbols used in ceremonies and rituals. Picture a Paint Clan member carefully painting intricate designs on a ceremonial drum, their artistry adding beauty and significance to the object. Their creative contributions enhance the cultural and spiritual life of the village.

Each clan has its own leader, often referred to as a clan mother or elder. These leaders provide guidance, support, and representation for their clan members. They play a crucial role in maintaining the social structure and ensuring that the traditions and values of the clan are upheld. Imagine a clan mother advising a young woman on her responsibilities within the clan, helping her understand her role and how she can contribute to the community. The wisdom and experience of the clan leaders are invaluable in guiding their clan members and fostering a sense of belonging and continuity.

The clan system also plays a significant role in social interactions and relationships. For example, marriage within the same clan is traditionally forbidden, ensuring that families are connected through a network of alliances and relationships with other clans. This practice helps maintain genetic diversity and strengthens the bonds between different clans. Imagine a wedding ceremony where members of different clans come together to celebrate the union, their ties and relationships reinforcing the unity of the village.

The clan system extends beyond social and familial relationships to include responsibilities in ceremonies and rituals. Each clan has specific roles and duties during festivals and important events. For example, the Bird Clan might be responsible for leading the spiritual aspects of a ceremony, while the Deer Clan provides the food. Picture a Green Corn Ceremony where each clan contributes its unique skills and knowledge, working together to ensure a successful and meaningful celebration. The cooperation and coordination among the clans reflect the interconnectedness and interdependence of the community.

The clan system also fosters a sense of identity and pride among its members. Being part of a clan connects individuals to their ancestors and heritage, providing a sense of continuity and belonging. Imagine a child learning about the history and traditions of their clan from their elders, understanding the legacy they are part of and the values they are expected to uphold. This sense of identity helps strengthen the cultural fabric of the community, ensuring that traditions and values are passed down through generations.

importance of clans in social structure and marriage

In the Cherokee clan system, each member has a specific role to play, contributing to the overall well-being of the village. For instance, members of the Deer Clan might be known for their hunting skills, providing food for the community. Members of the Blue Clan might serve as healers, using their knowledge of medicinal plants to care for the sick. Picture a village where everyone knows their responsibilities and works together seamlessly, each person's contributions valued and appreciated.

The clan system also ensures that everyone in the community has support and guidance. Clan leaders, often referred to as clan mothers or elders, provide advice and resolve conflicts within the clan. These leaders are respected for their wisdom and experience, and their guidance helps maintain harmony within the clan and the broader community. Imagine seeking counsel from a clan mother, her wise words helping you navigate a difficult decision or resolve a dispute.

One of the most important functions of the clan system is its role in marriage practices. In Cherokee society, marriage within the same clan is traditionally forbidden. This practice, known as exogamy, ensures that clans are interconnected through a network of alliances and relationships with other clans. By marrying outside their clan, individuals help create bonds between different clans, strengthening the unity and cohesion of the village. Imagine the joy and excitement of a wedding where members from different clans come together to celebrate, their connections reinforcing the fabric of the community.

Exogamy also has practical benefits. By marrying into other clans, individuals help maintain genetic diversity, which is important for the health and resilience of the population. This practice reduces the risk of inherited diseases and contributes to the overall strength and vitality of the community. Picture the children born from these unions, carrying the combined heritage of their parents' clans and benefiting from a diverse genetic background.

Marriage is a significant event in Cherokee society, marked by various customs and ceremonies. The involvement of clans in these ceremonies reinforces the importance of the clan system and the connections it creates. Imagine a wedding ceremony where the bride and groom's clans play active roles, each contributing their unique traditions and practices. The presence of clan leaders and members adds a layer of meaning and significance to the event, symbolizing the union not just of two individuals, but of two families and clans.

The process of choosing a marriage partner involves careful consideration of clan affiliations. Families and clan leaders often play a role in these decisions, ensuring that the match is beneficial for both individuals and their clans. Imagine the discussions and negotiations that take place, with families seeking to form alliances that will strengthen their clans and benefit the community. These decisions are made with an eye toward the future, considering the well-being of both the couple and the broader village.

Once a marriage is agreed upon, the wedding ceremony

itself is a vibrant and joyous celebration. It typically includes rituals and customs that reflect the cultural values and traditions of the Cherokee people. Picture the bride and groom dressed in traditional attire, adorned with symbols of their clans, standing before their families and community members. The ceremony might include prayers, songs, and dances, each element chosen to honor the couple and their union.

The involvement of the clans in the wedding ceremony reinforces the social structure and the importance of communal support. Clan members offer blessings and gifts, symbolizing their commitment to supporting the couple in their new life together. Imagine the sense of community and shared responsibility as the clans come together to celebrate, their participation strengthening the bonds between them.

After the wedding, the new couple continues to play their roles within their respective clans, but now they also have a new set of responsibilities to each other and their new family unit. The support and guidance of their clans remain crucial as they navigate this new phase of life. Picture the couple working together, drawing on the strengths and traditions of their clans to build a strong and harmonious family.

The importance of the clan system extends beyond social and marital functions; it also plays a crucial role in maintaining cultural continuity. Through the clans, cultural knowledge, traditions, and values are passed down from one generation to the next. Imagine a child learning about their clan's history and customs from their elders, understanding their place within the community and the responsibilities they will one day inherit. This transmission of knowledge ensures that the cultural heritage of the Cherokee people is preserved and celebrated.

The clan system also fosters a sense of collective identity and belonging. Being part of a clan connects individuals to their ancestors and provides a sense of continuity and stability. Imagine the pride and connection you would feel knowing that you are part of a long line of clan members, each contributing to the community in their unique way. This sense of identity helps strengthen the cultural fabric of the village, creating a community where everyone knows their place and their purpose.

In times of crisis, the clan system provides a network of support and solidarity. Clan members come together to help those in need, whether it's providing food, care, or emotional support. Imagine a village facing a difficult winter, with clans working together to ensure that everyone has enough to eat and that the vulnerable are cared for. The strength and resilience of the clan system help the community navigate challenges and emerge stronger.

5 / cherokee beliefs and spirituality

overview of cherokee spiritual beliefs

CENTRAL TO CHEROKEE spirituality is the belief in a Great Spirit, often referred to as Unetlanvhi, which means "Creator" or "Great Spirit." This supreme being is considered the source of all life and the force that sustains the universe. Imagine the reverence and awe the Cherokee feel for Unetlanvhi, seeing this presence in every aspect of the natural world—from the towering trees and flowing rivers to the smallest plants and animals. This belief fosters a deep respect for all living things and a commitment to living in harmony with nature.

Cherokee spirituality also encompasses a belief in a complex world of spirits and supernatural beings that inhabit the natural world. These spirits can be found in animals, plants, rocks, and other natural elements. For example, the Eagle is revered for its strength and connection to the heavens, while the Bear is respected for its power and healing abilities. Imagine the Cherokee observing the behavior of animals, seeing them as messengers and guides, and seeking their wisdom in times of need.

One important aspect of Cherokee spirituality is the

concept of balance and harmony. The Cherokee believe that maintaining balance within oneself, the community, and the natural world is essential for health and well-being. This idea is reflected in many of their rituals and ceremonies, which aim to restore and maintain this balance. Picture a Cherokee healer performing a ritual to cleanse a person's spirit, using herbs and prayers to bring harmony back to their body and soul.

The Cherokee also have a rich tradition of creation stories and legends that explain the origins of the world and the place of humans within it. These stories are not just tales of the past; they are living narratives that convey important spiritual and moral lessons. One such story is the Cherokee creation myth, which tells of how the earth was formed on the back of a giant turtle and how the first humans were created. Imagine listening to an elder recount this story, the vivid imagery painting a picture of the world's beginnings and the interconnectedness of all life.

Another key element of Cherokee spirituality is the practice of ceremonies and rituals that mark important events and transitions in life. These ceremonies often involve music, dance, and the use of sacred objects. For example, the Green Corn Ceremony is a major event that celebrates the beginning of the corn harvest. It is a time of renewal and purification, where the community comes together to give thanks for the harvest and to cleanse themselves of any negativity. Picture the villagers gathered around a sacred fire, singing and dancing, their movements synchronized with the rhythm of the drums and the chanting of prayers.

The Cherokee also use sacred objects in their spiritual practices. One such object is the medicine bag, a small pouch that contains items believed to have spiritual power, such as herbs, stones, or animal parts. Each person's medicine bag is unique, reflecting their personal spiritual journey and the guidance they seek. Imagine a Cherokee person carrying their medicine bag with them, feeling the comfort and protection of the sacred objects inside, each one chosen for its special significance.

Dreams and visions play a significant role in Cherokee spirituality. They are seen as a way to receive messages from the spirit world and to gain insight into one's life and purpose. The Cherokee often seek guidance through vision quests, which involve spending time alone in nature, fasting, and praying to receive a vision. Picture a young Cherokee embarking on a vision quest, journeying into the wilderness with a deep sense of purpose, seeking answers and clarity from the spirits.

Healing practices are another vital aspect of Cherokee spirituality. The Cherokee have a deep knowledge of medicinal plants and use them in their healing rituals. This knowledge is passed down through generations, with healers learning the properties and uses of various plants from their elders. Imagine a Cherokee healer gathering herbs from the forest, their knowledge guiding them to the right plants, and preparing remedies to treat the ailments of their community. Healing practices often involve not just the physical treatment but also the spiritual, addressing the whole person.

The Cherokee also believe in the power of prayer and song to connect with the spiritual world. Prayers are offered for various purposes, such as asking for guidance, giving thanks, or seeking protection. Songs, often accompanied by drums and rattles, are used in ceremonies and rituals to invoke the presence of the spirits. Picture a Cherokee ceremony where the air is filled with the sound of drumming and singing, each note and beat resonating with spiritual energy, creating a sacred space for the community to connect with the divine.

The clan system, which is central to Cherokee social structure, also plays a significant role in their spiritual beliefs. Each clan has its own spiritual traditions and responsibilities, and members often turn to their clan leaders for spiritual guidance. Imagine a clan mother leading her clan in a ritual, her knowledge and wisdom guiding them in their spiritual practices. The clan system reinforces the sense of community and interconnectedness, with each clan contributing to the spiritual life of the village.

The Cherokee also have specific rituals for different life stages, such as birth, puberty, marriage, and death. These rituals help individuals navigate the transitions of life, providing spiritual support and guidance. For example, the naming ceremony for a newborn is a significant event where the child is given a name that reflects their place in the community and their spiritual path. Picture the parents holding their baby as the elder performs the naming ceremony, the community gathered to welcome the new life and offer their blessings.

Death and the afterlife are also important aspects of Cherokee spirituality. The Cherokee believe in an afterlife where the spirit continues its journey. Funerary practices are designed to honor the deceased and to ensure their safe passage to the spirit world. Imagine a funeral ceremony where the community gathers to pay their respects, offering prayers and songs to guide the departed spirit. These practices reflect the Cherokee belief in the continuity of life and the enduring connection between the living and the dead.

Throughout all these practices, the underlying theme is the interconnectedness of all things. The Cherokee see themselves as part of a larger web of life, where every action and decision has an impact on the whole. This perspective fosters a deep sense of responsibility and respect for the natural world and for each other. Imagine the daily life of a Cherokee person, where every action—from the way they treat the land to the way they interact with others—is guided by this understanding of interconnectedness.

connection to nature and the land

The Cherokee view the land as a living entity, imbued with spirit and vitality. This belief fosters a profound respect for the environment and a commitment to living in harmony with nature. Imagine a Cherokee elder teaching children about the land, explaining that every rock, tree, and stream has its own spirit and purpose. This understanding instills a sense of reverence and responsibility, encouraging the community to care for the land as they would for a family member.

One of the central tenets of Cherokee spirituality is the concept of balance and harmony, which extends to their relationship with the land. The Cherokee believe that maintaining balance within themselves and with the natural world is essential for health and well-being. This belief is reflected in their agricultural practices, hunting rituals, and the way they interact with the environment. Picture a Cherokee farmer planting crops using traditional methods that ensure the soil remains fertile and the ecosystem stays healthy. These sustainable practices are a testament to their commitment to preserving the land for future generations.

The Cherokee also have a deep understanding of the seasons and cycles of nature. They celebrate the changing seasons with various festivals and ceremonies that honor the earth's rhythms. For example, the Green Corn Ceremony marks the beginning of the corn harvest and is a time of thanksgiving and renewal. Imagine the community coming together to celebrate this festival, giving thanks for the bounty of the earth and participating in rituals to ensure continued prosperity. The ceremony involves songs, dances, and offerings, all designed to honor the spirits of the land and to express gratitude for the harvest.

Hunting and fishing are integral parts of Cherokee life, and these activities are conducted with great respect for the animals and the environment. The Cherokee believe that animals are sentient beings with their own spirits and that hunting should be done with humility and gratitude. Imagine a group of Cherokee hunters preparing for a hunt, offering prayers and rituals to honor the spirit of the animal they seek. They use every part of the animal, ensuring nothing goes to waste, and they thank the animal's spirit for its sacrifice. This respectful approach to hunting reflects their deep connection to nature and their understanding of the interconnectedness of all life.

Fishing practices are similarly conducted with respect and care. The Cherokee use traditional methods, such as fish weirs and traps, that allow them to catch fish sustainably. Picture a Cherokee family by the river, setting up a fish weir with careful attention to the flow of the water and the behavior of the fish. This method ensures that they catch enough fish to feed the community without depleting the river's resources. The Cherokee's knowledge of the natural world and their sustainable practices help maintain the balance of the ecosystem.

Gathering wild plants and herbs is another important aspect of Cherokee life. The Cherokee have an extensive knowledge of the plants in their environment and use them for food, medicine, and other purposes. Imagine a Cherokee healer walking through the forest, identifying and gathering medicinal plants with a deep understanding of their properties and uses. This knowledge is passed down through generations, ensuring that the community can continue to benefit from the natural resources around them. The practice of gathering is done with respect for the plants, taking only what is needed and leaving enough for the plants to regenerate.

The Cherokee also express their connection to nature through their art and craftsmanship. Traditional crafts, such as basket weaving, pottery, and beadwork, often incorporate natural materials and reflect the natural world. Imagine a Cherokee artisan weaving a basket from river cane, their hands moving deftly to create intricate patterns that mimic the shapes and forms found in nature. These crafts are not just functional; they are also a way to honor the beauty and diversity of the natural world.

Storytelling is another way the Cherokee connect with nature. Many Cherokee legends and myths feature animals, plants, and natural elements as central characters, conveying important lessons about living in harmony with the environment. Imagine an elder sitting by a fire, telling a story about how the possum got its bare tail or why the owl has big eyes. These stories are more than just entertainment; they are a means of teaching the community about the natural world and the importance of respecting it.

Ceremonies and rituals also play a crucial role in the Cherokee's connection to nature. Many of these practices are designed to honor the spirits of the land and to seek their guidance and blessings. For example, the Cherokee might perform a water blessing ceremony to purify and honor a river, acknowledging its importance to their survival and well-being. Picture the community gathered by the river, offering prayers and songs, and placing sacred objects in the water as a sign of respect and gratitude. These ceremonies reinforce the bond between the Cherokee people and the natural world, reminding them of their place within the larger web of life.

The connection to nature is also evident in the Cherokee's daily routines and practices. They live in harmony with the land, using natural resources in ways that are sustainable and respectful. Imagine a Cherokee family building a home using traditional materials and methods that blend seamlessly with the environment. Their homes are designed to be in tune with the natural surroundings, providing shelter while minimizing their impact on the land.

role of medicine men and women

Medicine men and women are often chosen based on their innate abilities and their dedication to learning the ancient practices passed down through generations. They undergo rigorous training, learning from elders who share their knowledge of medicinal plants, healing rituals, and spiritual practices. Imagine a young apprentice spending years studying under a skilled medicine man or woman, walking through forests to gather herbs, and learning the secrets of healing through observation and practice.

The role of medicine men and women is multifaceted, encompassing physical, spiritual, and emotional healing. One of their primary responsibilities is to treat illnesses and injuries using natural remedies. They have an extensive knowledge of the medicinal properties of plants and know how to prepare and administer these remedies effectively. Picture a medicine woman carefully selecting herbs from a forest, her keen eye identifying the plants that will be used to create a healing salve or tea. She combines these herbs with precise skill, creating remedies that can alleviate pain, reduce inflammation, or cure infections.

In addition to their knowledge of herbal medicine, medicine men and women also perform healing rituals that address the spiritual aspects of health. The Cherokee believe that illness can be caused by spiritual imbalances, negative energy, or disharmony with nature. Medicine men and women use rituals, prayers, and ceremonies to restore balance and harmony. Imagine a medicine man performing a healing ceremony, his chants resonating with spiritual power as he invokes the assistance of the spirits to cleanse and heal the afflicted person. These rituals often involve the use of sacred objects, such as feathers, stones, and herbs, each chosen for its specific spiritual significance.

Medicine men and women also play a vital role in guiding the community through important life transitions. They perform ceremonies for births, deaths, and other significant events, ensuring that these transitions are marked with respect and spiritual guidance. Picture a medicine woman conducting a naming ceremony for a newborn, blessing the child and invoking the protection of the spirits. Her words and actions help integrate the child into the community, connecting them to their heritage and the natural world.

Another important aspect of their role is the interpretation of dreams and visions. The Cherokee believe that dreams are a way for the spirit world to communicate with the living, offering guidance and insight. Medicine men and women are skilled in interpreting these messages, helping individuals understand the significance of their dreams and how they relate to their lives. Imagine someone coming to a medicine man with a vivid dream, seeking his interpretation. The medicine man listens carefully, using his knowledge and intuition to unravel the meaning of the dream and provide valuable advice.

Medicine men and women are also educators, passing on their knowledge to the next generation. They teach young apprentices about medicinal plants, healing techniques, and spiritual practices, ensuring that this vital knowledge is preserved. Picture a group of apprentices gathered around a medicine woman, listening intently as she explains the properties of a particular herb and demonstrates how to prepare it. Through their teachings, medicine men and women help maintain the cultural heritage and health of the community.

In times of crisis, medicine men and women offer support and guidance to the community. Whether it's a natural disaster, an epidemic, or a conflict, they provide the wisdom and healing needed to navigate these challenges. Imagine a village struck by an illness, with the medicine man working tirelessly to care for the sick, preparing remedies, and performing healing rituals. His presence provides comfort and hope, reinforcing the community's resilience and unity.

The role of medicine men and women extends beyond individual healing; they are also stewards of the land. Their deep knowledge of the environment and its resources helps the community live sustainably and in harmony with nature. They advocate for practices that protect and preserve the natural world, understanding that the health of the land is directly connected to the health of the people. Imagine a medicine woman leading a group through the forest, teaching them about the importance of conservation and showing them how to gather plants respectfully and sustainably.

Medicine men and women are also counselors, offering advice and support for personal and communal issues. They help resolve conflicts, provide guidance on personal matters, and offer spiritual counseling. Picture a couple seeking the advice of a medicine man to strengthen their relationship, or a young person looking for guidance on their life path. The medicine man listens with empathy and offers wisdom that helps individuals navigate their challenges and find solutions.

Their role is one of service and sacrifice, dedicated to the well-being of others. Medicine men and women often put the needs of the community above their own, working tirelessly to ensure that everyone is cared for. They embody the values of compassion, humility, and respect, serving as role models for the entire community. Imagine the deep respect and gratitude the village feels for their medicine men and women, knowing that their dedication and skills are vital to their survival and well-being.

traditional healing practices and herbal medicine

Herbal medicine is a cornerstone of traditional Cherokee healing. Medicine men and women are skilled in identifying, gathering, and preparing a wide variety of plants for medicinal use. Imagine a healer walking through the forest, their keen eyes spotting the plants they need. They might gather yellow root for its antibiotic properties, or boneset to treat fever and colds. Each plant is selected with care, and the healer offers a prayer of thanks for its healing power.

Once gathered, the plants are prepared using methods that have been passed down through generations. Some herbs are dried and ground into powders, while others are made into teas, poultices, or salves. Picture a medicine woman in her home, carefully drying herbs on racks and grinding them with a stone mortar and pestle. The preparation of these remedies is done with precision and respect, ensuring that the full medicinal properties of the plants are preserved.

One common herbal remedy used by the Cherokee is tea made from wild cherry bark. This tea is known for its ability to soothe coughs and sore throats. Imagine the soothing process of making this tea: the bark is carefully stripped from the tree, dried, and then steeped in hot water. The resulting tea is not only effective but also a comforting, warm drink that brings relief to the patient.

Another important plant in Cherokee medicine is black cohosh, which is used to treat a variety of ailments, including menstrual cramps, arthritis, and snake bites. The root of the black cohosh plant is harvested, dried, and used to make a strong tea or tincture. Picture a healer preparing a batch of black cohosh tea, knowing that it will provide relief and healing to those in need.

Traditional Cherokee healing practices also involve the use of poultices and salves. A poultice is made by crushing fresh herbs and applying them directly to the skin to draw out infection or reduce inflammation. For example, a poultice made from plantain leaves can be used to treat cuts, insect bites, and skin infections. Imagine the cool, soothing sensation as the poultice is applied to a wound, the natural properties of the plant working to heal and protect the skin.

Salves are made by infusing herbs in oil and then combining the oil with beeswax to create a thick, healing balm. These salves are used to treat a variety of skin conditions, from burns and rashes to dry, cracked skin. Picture a medicine man stirring a pot of herb-infused oil over a fire, carefully adding the beeswax and pouring the mixture into small containers. These salves are treasured remedies, used by families to treat everyday ailments.

Beyond physical remedies, traditional Cherokee healing practices also address the spiritual and emotional aspects of health. The Cherokee believe that illness can be caused by imbalances in the spirit or disruptions in harmony with nature. To address these issues, healers use rituals, prayers, and ceremonies to restore balance and promote healing. Imagine a healing ceremony where a medicine woman uses smoke from burning sage to cleanse a person's spirit, her chants and prayers calling on the spirits for assistance.

One such ceremony is the "going to water" ritual, which involves immersing oneself in a river or stream to cleanse the body and spirit. This ritual is often performed at dawn, when the water is believed to be most powerful. Picture a group of people wading into a cool, clear stream as the sun begins to rise, their hands scooping water over their heads as they pray for healing and purification. This ritual reflects the deep connection between the Cherokee and the natural world, and the belief in the healing power of water.

Dream interpretation is another important aspect of Cherokee healing. Dreams are seen as messages from the spirit world, offering guidance and insight. Healers are skilled in interpreting these dreams, helping individuals understand their significance and how they relate to their health and well-being. Imagine someone describing a vivid dream to a medicine man, who listens carefully and then explains the symbols and messages within the dream. This practice helps individuals gain a deeper understanding of their spiritual health and how it affects their physical and emotional well-being.

The use of sweat lodges is another traditional practice used to promote healing and purification. A sweat lodge is a small, dome-shaped structure made from natural materials, where individuals gather to sweat out toxins and cleanse their bodies. The heat and steam from the sweat lodge are believed to open the pores, release impurities, and promote healing. Picture the intense, cleansing heat of the sweat lodge, as people sit together, sweating and praying, their bodies and spirits being purified.

Music and dance are also integral to Cherokee healing practices. Certain songs and dances are believed to have healing properties, invoking the spirits and promoting harmony. Imagine a healing dance, where participants move rhythmically to the beat of drums, their movements synchronized with the music. The energy of the dance, combined with the power of the music, creates a powerful healing experience.

The holistic approach to healing in Cherokee tradition emphasizes the interconnectedness of all aspects of life. Physical health, emotional well-being, and spiritual balance are all seen as interrelated, and treatment often involves addressing all these aspects together. This holistic view is reflected in the healer's approach to diagnosis and treatment. Imagine a medicine woman taking the time to talk with a patient, understanding their physical symptoms as well as their emotional state and spiritual health. This comprehensive understanding allows her to create a treatment plan that addresses the root causes of illness, not just the symptoms.

The role of the healer in Cherokee society is not just to treat illness, but to educate and empower individuals to take care of their own health. Healers teach their communities about the medicinal properties of plants, healthy living practices, and ways to maintain balance and harmony in their lives. Picture a healer leading a workshop on herbal medicine, showing community members how to identify and use local plants for healing. Through this education, the healer helps ensure that traditional knowledge is passed down and that the community can continue to thrive.

6 / the trail of tears

events leading up to the trail of tears

THE CHEROKEE PEOPLE WERE THRIVING, their communities are strong, and they have adapted to many changes while maintaining their cultural identity. However, a series of events are unfolding that will profoundly impact their lives and lead to one of the most tragic chapters in their history: the Trail of Tears.

The story begins with the increasing pressure from European settlers and the United States government to acquire Cherokee lands. The Cherokee homeland, rich in resources and strategically located, becomes highly desirable to the growing nation. Picture the lush forests, fertile fields, and abundant wildlife that make the Cherokee territory so valuable. As settlers push westward, they covet this land for farming, mining, and expansion.

In response to these pressures, the Cherokee take significant steps to adapt and coexist with the settlers. They adopt many aspects of European-American culture, including creating a written language, establishing a constitution, and developing a more centralized government. Imagine Sequoyah, a Cherokee silversmith, dedicating years to develop the Cherokee syllabary, a written system that enables the Cherokee people to read and write in their own language. This achievement is monumental, empowering the Cherokee to publish newspapers and legal documents, thereby strengthening their nation.

Despite these efforts to assimilate and protect their land, the pressure continues to mount. In 1828, gold is discovered in northern Georgia, within Cherokee territory, intensifying the demand for their land. Imagine the excitement and greed that grips the settlers and prospectors, eager to strike it rich. The Georgia government, determined to claim the gold-rich lands, passes laws to extend state authority over Cherokee territory, effectively nullifying Cherokee sovereignty.

The situation becomes even more dire with the election of President Andrew Jackson in 1828. Jackson is a strong proponent of westward expansion and has little regard for Native American rights. Picture a fiery and determined Andrew Jackson, advocating for the removal of Native Americans to clear the way for settlers. In 1830, Jackson signs the Indian Removal Act into law, authorizing the forced relocation of Native American tribes living east of the Mississippi River to lands west of the river.

The Cherokee nation, under the leadership of Principal Chief John Ross, fights tirelessly to resist removal. They take their case to the U.S. Supreme Court, resulting in the landmark case Worcester v. Georgia in 1832. The Court rules in favor of the Cherokee, affirming their sovereign rights and declaring Georgia's actions unconstitutional. Imagine the sense of hope and justice felt by the Cherokee people as they hear the Supreme Court's decision. However, President Jackson refuses to enforce the ruling, famously defying the Court and continuing his removal policy.

Amidst this turmoil, a faction within the Cherokee nation, led by Major Ridge, his son John Ridge, and Elias Boudinot, believes that removal is inevitable and that negotiating a treaty is the best way to protect their people. They secretly sign the

Treaty of New Echota in 1835, ceding all Cherokee land east of the Mississippi River in exchange for land in present-day Oklahoma and financial compensation. Picture the tension and conflict within the Cherokee community, as many view the signers of the treaty as traitors who have betrayed their nation.

Chief John Ross and the majority of the Cherokee people vehemently oppose the treaty, arguing that it does not represent the will of the Cherokee nation. Ross gathers thousands of signatures in a petition to Congress, urging them to reject the treaty. Imagine John Ross, a determined and passionate leader, tirelessly advocating for his people, traveling to Washington, D.C., to present the petition. Despite their efforts, the U.S. Senate ratifies the Treaty of New Echota by a single vote in 1836.

With the treaty ratified, the stage is set for the forced removal of the Cherokee people. The U.S. government begins preparing for the relocation, and the Cherokee are given a deadline to voluntarily move west. Most refuse, clinging to their homes and hoping for a reprieve. Picture the Cherokee families tending to their fields, children playing in the villages, all unaware of the impending devastation.

In May 1838, the deadline passes, and the U.S. military, under the command of General Winfield Scott, begins forcibly rounding up the Cherokee. Soldiers enter Cherokee homes, dragging people out, often with only the clothes on their backs. Imagine the chaos and heartbreak as families are torn from their land, homes destroyed, and communities shattered. Thousands of Cherokee are herded into makeshift camps, where they await the long and arduous journey west.

As the Cherokee are marched westward in what becomes known as the Trail of Tears, they face unimaginable hardships. The journey is grueling, covering over 1,000 miles through harsh conditions. Many travel on foot, while others are crammed into overcrowded wagons. Picture the long lines of Cherokee men, women, and children, walking through rain, snow, and scorching heat, with little food or shelter. Disease, starvation, and exposure take a terrible toll, and thousands die along the way.

The Trail of Tears is not just a physical journey but a devastating emotional and spiritual ordeal. The Cherokee are forced to leave behind their ancestral homeland, the graves of their ancestors, and the land that has sustained them for generations. Imagine the deep sorrow and sense of loss as they are driven from their homes, their way of life forever changed.

impact of the indian removal act

The Indian Removal Act, signed into law by President Andrew Jackson in 1830, marked the beginning of a painful and transformative period for the Cherokee and other Native American tribes. This act authorized the U.S. government to negotiate treaties with Native American tribes to relocate them west of the Mississippi River. The government's aim was to open up their ancestral lands for white settlers. Imagine the anxiety and fear that gripped the Cherokee community as they realized the implications of this new policy.

One of the most immediate impacts of the Indian Removal Act was the erosion of the Cherokee's sovereignty. Despite the Cherokee Nation's efforts to assimilate and coexist with the settlers by adopting a written language, creating a constitution, and engaging in legal battles, their sovereignty was continually undermined. Picture Chief John Ross and other Cherokee leaders tirelessly fighting to protect their people's rights and land through diplomatic and legal means, only to see their efforts repeatedly thwarted by an unsympathetic government.

The passage of the Indian Removal Act intensified the pressure on the Cherokee to leave their land. Many Cherokee families lived in fear and uncertainty, unsure of what the future would hold. Imagine a family sitting around their evening fire, parents trying to reassure their children while secretly fearing the loss of their home and way of life. This fear was compounded by the aggressive actions of state governments like Georgia, which passed laws that extended state jurisdiction over Cherokee lands and nullified their legal rights.

The situation became even more dire with the signing of the Treaty of New Echota in 1835. This treaty, signed by a small faction of the Cherokee without the consent of the majority or the approval of the Cherokee government, ceded all Cherokee lands east of the Mississippi River in exchange for land in present-day Oklahoma and other concessions. Imagine the betrayal felt by the majority of the Cherokee people, who saw the treaty as illegitimate and fought against its enforcement. Chief John Ross collected thousands of signatures on a petition to Congress, protesting the treaty and pleading for justice.

Despite these efforts, the U.S. government ratified the Treaty of New Echota, and preparations for the forced removal began. The impact on the Cherokee community was devastating. Soldiers began rounding up Cherokee families, often with little warning, forcing them from their homes and into makeshift camps. Picture the chaos and heartbreak as families were torn from their land, homes were destroyed, and cherished possessions were left behind.

The forced march westward, known as the Trail of Tears, resulted in immense suffering and loss. Approximately 16,000 Cherokee were forced to leave their homes and undertake a grueling journey of over 1,000 miles. The journey was marked by harsh conditions, disease, and inadequate supplies. Imagine the long lines of men, women, and children walking through harsh weather, with little food or shelter. Many fell ill and died along the way, their bodies buried in shallow graves by the roadside.

The physical toll of the Trail of Tears was matched by the emotional and spiritual impact. The Cherokee were forced to leave behind not only their homes but also the graves of their ancestors and the land that held deep cultural and spiritual significance. Imagine the sorrow and sense of loss as they were uprooted from a place that was central to their identity and way of life. This forced displacement shattered communities and disrupted traditional ways of living.

Upon arriving in the unfamiliar territory of present-day Oklahoma, the Cherokee faced the daunting task of rebuilding their lives. The land was different, and they had to adapt to new conditions while still grieving the loss of their homeland. Imagine the resilience required to start over, to build new homes, plant new crops, and create new communities in an unfamiliar place. The Cherokee drew on their cultural strength and sense of community to rebuild, but the trauma of the removal lingered.

The impact of the Indian Removal Act extended beyond the immediate suffering and loss. It set a precedent for the treatment of Native American tribes by the U.S. government, leading to further displacement and marginalization of indigenous peoples. The policy of forced removal disrupted traditional ways of life, led to the loss of vast amounts of tribal land, and contributed to long-term economic and social challenges for Native American communities.

forced relocation

Imagine the peaceful morning in a Cherokee village, the sun rising over the mountains and casting a warm glow on the land. The villagers are going about their daily routines, unaware that their lives are about to be turned upside down. Suddenly, soldiers arrive, disrupting the calm with orders to gather everyone immediately. The forced relocation, which we now know as the Trail of Tears, is about to begin.

The soldiers, acting on orders from the U.S. government, begin the process of rounding up the Cherokee people from their homes. Picture the confusion and fear as families are given little time to pack their belongings. The soldiers are often harsh, providing minimal explanation and showing little empathy for the distress they are causing. Imagine being told to leave your home with only what you can carry, knowing you may never return.

The Cherokee are herded into makeshift forts and camps, where they are held until the relocation begins. These camps are overcrowded and lack adequate sanitation, leading to the spread of disease. Imagine the conditions in these camps: families huddled together, trying to find some semblance of comfort and dignity amidst the chaos. The elders, who are often the keepers of tradition and history, try to reassure the younger ones, but the uncertainty weighs heavily on everyone.

As the time for departure approaches, the Cherokee are organized into groups for the long journey west. The U.S. government has planned multiple routes, but none are easy. Some groups will travel by land, others by river, but all face grueling conditions. Picture the long lines of Cherokee people, men, women, and children, beginning their journey. They are forced to walk for miles each day, often through difficult terrain and harsh weather.

The land routes are particularly arduous. The Cherokee must traverse mountains, cross rivers, and walk through dense forests. Imagine the physical toll of this journey: feet blistered and sore, muscles aching, and the relentless fatigue that comes from walking day after day. The elderly and the very young suffer the most, their bodies unable to withstand the strain. Many fall ill along the way, and there are few provisions for medical care.

For those traveling by river, the conditions are no better. They are crowded onto flatboats and barges, navigating rivers that are often treacherous. Imagine the cold, damp conditions on these boats, with little shelter from the elements. Food and clean water are scarce, and disease spreads quickly in the cramped quarters. The constant movement of the boat adds to the discomfort and makes it difficult for the sick and elderly to rest.

The Cherokee are provided with inadequate supplies for the journey. The food is often spoiled or insufficient, leading to malnutrition. Imagine trying to sustain yourself on meager rations while expending so much energy each day. Water sources are often contaminated, and clean drinking water is hard to come by. The lack of basic necessities adds to the suffering and increases the mortality rate among the travelers.

The emotional toll of the journey is as severe as the physical hardships. The Cherokee are leaving behind not just their homes, but their way of life. The land they are forced to abandon holds deep cultural and spiritual significance. Imagine the sorrow of passing familiar landmarks, knowing that this is the last time you will see them. The psychological burden of losing one's home and heritage weighs heavily on everyone.

Despite the suffering, the Cherokee display remarkable resilience and solidarity. Families support each other, sharing what little they have and offering comfort in times of need. Imagine the moments of quiet strength: a mother soothing her child with a lullaby, an elder telling stories to keep the spirits up, and friends encouraging each other to keep going. These acts of kindness and community help sustain them through the darkest times.

As the journey progresses, the weather becomes a significant adversary. The Cherokee endure extreme heat in the summer and bitter cold in the winter. Imagine walking through snow and ice, with inadequate clothing to keep warm, or enduring the scorching heat without sufficient water. Many succumb to the elements, their bodies unable to cope with the harsh conditions.

The journey westward takes several months, and for many, it becomes a journey of survival. Death is a constant companion, with thousands of Cherokee perishing from disease, exposure, and exhaustion. Imagine the heartbreak of losing loved ones along the way, unable to give them a proper burial, and knowing that their graves are left unmarked in a foreign land.

Despite the unimaginable hardships, the Cherokee maintain their cultural identity and traditions. They continue to practice their rituals, sing their songs, and tell their stories. Imagine a campfire at night, where families gather to share food, tell stories, and pray for strength. These moments of cultural continuity provide solace and help preserve their identity in the face of adversity.

Finally, after months of suffering, the surviving Cherokee reach the designated Indian Territory, in what is now Oklahoma. The land is unfamiliar and often unwelcoming, far from the lush forests and mountains of their homeland. Imagine the sense of displacement and uncertainty as they try to rebuild their lives in this new environment. They must start from scratch, building new homes, planting new crops, and re-establishing their community.

how the cherokee rebuilt their communities

The Cherokee's strong sense of community and organization played a crucial role in their recovery. They quickly came together to divide tasks and responsibilities, ensuring that everyone contributed to the rebuilding efforts. Picture groups of men clearing land and constructing homes, while women gathered food and cared for the children. This collective effort created a sense of purpose and unity, helping to heal the emotional wounds of the past months.

One of the first steps in rebuilding was to establish new homes. The Cherokee used traditional building techniques, adapting them to the materials available in their new environment. Imagine the process of constructing wattle and daub houses, with men weaving branches together to form a sturdy frame, while women mixed clay and straw to create walls. These homes were simple but functional, providing much-needed shelter and a sense of stability.

Agriculture was another critical aspect of their survival. The Cherokee were skilled farmers, and they quickly began to clear fields and plant crops. They relied on their knowledge of the Three Sisters—corn, beans, and squash—crops that grow well together and provide balanced nutrition. Picture the fields coming to life with green shoots, a hopeful sign of food to come. This agricultural work not only provided sustenance but also restored a sense of normalcy and routine.

Rebuilding their communities also meant reestablishing their governance and social structures. The Cherokee had a sophisticated system of government, with a constitution, councils, and leaders who were respected and trusted. Imagine Chief John Ross and other leaders holding meetings to discuss the future, their voices filled with determination and hope. They worked tirelessly to create new governmental structures that would ensure the well-being and representation of their people in their new home.

Education was another priority for the Cherokee. They understood the importance of educating their children and preserving their language and culture. Imagine the establishment of schools, where children learned to read and write in both Cherokee and English. Teachers, many of whom were community members, instilled a sense of pride in their heritage while preparing the younger generation for the future. These schools became centers of learning and cultural preservation, ensuring that the Cherokee identity would endure.

The Cherokee also reestablished their spiritual and cultural practices, which were essential to their sense of identity and community. Ceremonies, dances, and storytelling were revived, providing a way to honor their ancestors and connect with their heritage. Imagine a communal gathering around a fire, where elders told stories of their history and traditions, passing down wisdom to the younger generations. These cultural practices offered comfort and continuity, helping the Cherokee to heal and move forward.

Trade and commerce played a significant role in the rebuilding process. The Cherokee established trade networks with neighboring tribes and settlers, exchanging goods and services that were essential for their survival and economic stability. Picture bustling markets where Cherokee traders exchanged baskets, pottery, and agricultural produce for tools, fabrics, and other necessities. This commerce not only provided material support but also fostered relationships and mutual support with other communities.

Healthcare and traditional medicine were also critical components of rebuilding. The Cherokee relied on their knowledge of herbal medicine and healing practices to care for the sick and injured. Imagine a medicine woman preparing herbal remedies, her hands skilled and sure as she mixed plants into salves and teas. These traditional practices were complemented by new knowledge and techniques, creating a comprehensive approach to healthcare that served the community well.

Resilience and adaptability were key to the Cherokee's success in rebuilding their communities. They drew on their deep sense of identity, cultural heritage, and communal spirit to overcome the challenges they faced. Imagine the daily life in a newly rebuilt Cherokee village: children playing, elders sharing stories, families working together in the fields, and leaders planning for the future. This vibrant, resilient community was a testament to the strength and determination of the Cherokee people.

The rebuilding process was not without its difficulties. The Cherokee faced ongoing challenges, including conflicts with settlers and other tribes, economic hardships, and the struggle to maintain their sovereignty and rights. However, their strong sense of community and determination to preserve their culture helped them to navigate these obstacles. Imagine the resolve and tenacity required to advocate for their rights, to fight for their land and sovereignty, and to ensure that their voices were heard.

Sarah Michaels

lasting impact on the cherokee people

The Trail of Tears was not just a physical journey but an emotional and spiritual ordeal that left deep scars. The forced relocation caused tremendous loss: of life, homeland, and cultural continuity. This trauma has been passed down through generations, affecting the collective psyche of the Cherokee people. Imagine a grandmother telling her grandchildren about their ancestors' struggle, her voice heavy with the weight of history. This narrative of suffering and resilience is an integral part of Cherokee identity.

Despite the pain, the Cherokee have found ways to honor their past while looking toward the future. The preservation of language and culture has been a key focus. Imagine walking into a Cherokee language class, where children are learning to speak the words of their ancestors. Efforts to revive and maintain the Cherokee language are vital in keeping their heritage alive. Language is more than a means of communication; it is a connection to culture, history, and identity.

Cultural traditions, ceremonies, and stories continue to play a crucial role in Cherokee life. Picture a community gathering for the Green Corn Ceremony, a time-honored tradition that celebrates renewal and the harvest. This ceremony, like many others, is a way for the Cherokee to connect with their ancestors and the natural world. Through dance, song, and ritual, they honor their heritage and ensure that their cultural practices are passed on to future generations.

The impact of historical trauma is also seen in the social and economic challenges faced by the Cherokee people. The loss of their ancestral lands and the hardships of relocation disrupted their traditional way of life, leading to economic instability and social dislocation. However, the Cherokee have shown remarkable resilience in addressing these challenges. Imagine a modern Cherokee enterprise, where community members work together to create economic opportunities and build a sustainable future. These efforts reflect a commitment to self-determination and economic empowerment.

Education has been a cornerstone of the Cherokee's efforts to rebuild and thrive. The establishment of schools and institutions that teach both modern subjects and traditional knowledge is a testament to their dedication to learning and cultural preservation. Imagine students in a Cherokee school, learning about science and mathematics alongside the history and traditions of their people. This holistic approach to education ensures that the next generation is well-equipped to navigate the complexities of the modern world while staying rooted in their heritage.

Health and wellness are also areas where the lasting impact of the Trail of Tears is evident. The physical and psychological toll of forced relocation has had long-term effects on the health of the Cherokee people. However, traditional healing practices and modern healthcare initiatives are being combined to address these challenges. Picture a Cherokee health center where herbal medicine and modern treatments are used side by side, reflecting a holistic approach to health that honors traditional knowledge while embracing new advancements.

The Cherokee Nation's political structure has evolved to address contemporary issues while maintaining traditional governance principles. The re-establishment of a central government, complete with a constitution and elected officials, has been crucial in advocating for the rights and interests of the Cherokee people. Imagine a council meeting where leaders discuss policies and initiatives aimed at improving the community's well-being. This governance structure ensures that the Cherokee have a voice in decisions that affect their lives and their future.

Legal battles and advocacy have also been a significant part of the Cherokee's journey to reclaim their rights and protect their sovereignty. The fight for legal recognition and the enforcement of treaties continues to be a critical aspect of their struggle. Picture a courtroom where Cherokee lawyers and advocates passionately argue for their people's rights, drawing on both legal expertise and a deep sense of justice. These efforts are vital in ensuring that the promises made to the Cherokee are honored and that their sovereignty is respected.

Environmental stewardship is another area where the Cherokee have made a lasting impact. Their deep connection to the land and natural world informs their approach to environmental issues. Imagine a Cherokee environmental program that focuses on sustainable practices, conservation, and the protection of natural resources. This commitment to environmental stewardship reflects traditional values and is essential in addressing contemporary ecological challenges.

The resilience and adaptability of the Cherokee people are perhaps best exemplified by their cultural renaissance. Art, music, literature, and other forms of cultural expression are thriving, showcasing the vibrancy and creativity of the Cherokee community. Imagine a gallery filled with Cherokee art, each piece telling a story of heritage, survival, and hope. This cultural renaissance is a powerful reminder of the enduring spirit of the Cherokee people.

7 / modern cherokee life

life in modern cherokee communities

THIS CHAPTER EXPLORES what it is like to live in a contemporary Cherokee community, where tradition and innovation coexist harmoniously.

Start your morning in a Cherokee home, where families gather for breakfast. The meal might include traditional foods like corn mush or fry bread, alongside more modern options like cereal or eggs. Imagine the kitchen filled with the delicious aroma of freshly cooked food, and the sounds of family members chatting and preparing for the day ahead. This blend of traditional and contemporary elements is a hallmark of Cherokee life today.

Education is a cornerstone of modern Cherokee communities. Schools emphasize both academic excellence and cultural education, ensuring that children learn about their heritage as well as standard subjects like math and science. Picture a classroom where students are learning the Cherokee syllabary alongside English, guided by dedicated teachers who are passionate about preserving their language. In these schools, children not only gain knowledge but also a strong sense of identity and pride in their culture.

Technology plays a significant role in education and daily life. Imagine students using tablets and computers for their studies, accessing a wealth of information while staying connected to their cultural roots. Digital platforms are used to teach the Cherokee language, share traditional stories, and connect community members. This integration of technology helps bridge the gap between the past and the future, making learning more engaging and accessible.

Community centers are vital hubs of activity in Cherokee towns. These centers host various events, from cultural festivals and art exhibits to health clinics and job fairs. Imagine walking into a bustling community center where people are participating in a traditional dance workshop, learning to create beadwork, or attending a health seminar. These centers are places where the community comes together to celebrate, learn, and support one another.

Healthcare in Cherokee communities combines modern medical practices with traditional healing methods. Health clinics provide comprehensive care, including services from doctors and nurses, as well as traditional healers who use herbal medicine and spiritual practices. Picture a healthcare facility where a patient can receive a check-up from a nurse and then consult with a medicine man or woman for holistic treatment. This approach ensures that healthcare is both effective and culturally sensitive.

Economic development is another area where Cherokee communities are thriving. Many Cherokee-run businesses and enterprises contribute to the local economy, creating jobs and opportunities. Imagine a bustling market where artisans sell handcrafted jewelry, pottery, and other traditional crafts. These businesses not only support the economy but also help preserve cultural practices and skills.

Modern Cherokee governance is characterized by strong leadership and active participation from community members. The Cherokee Nation operates with a democratic government that includes a Principal Chief, a Tribal Council, and various departments that manage different aspects of community life. Imagine attending a council meeting where leaders discuss important issues, make decisions, and plan for the future. This democratic process ensures that the voices of the Cherokee people are heard and that their interests are represented.

Cultural preservation remains a central focus. Festivals, ceremonies, and other cultural events are regularly held to celebrate and maintain Cherokee traditions. The annual Cherokee National Holiday, for example, commemorates the signing of the Cherokee Constitution in 1839. Picture a vibrant festival with traditional music, dance, storytelling, and crafts, where people of all ages come together to honor their heritage. These events are crucial for keeping cultural practices alive and fostering a sense of community.

Art and music are thriving in modern Cherokee communities. Many artists and musicians draw inspiration from their heritage, creating works that reflect traditional themes while incorporating contemporary styles. Imagine a gallery showcasing Cherokee art, with paintings, sculptures, and textiles that tell stories of the past and present. Music performances might feature traditional instruments like flutes and drums alongside guitars and keyboards, creating a unique blend of sounds.

Environmental stewardship is another important aspect of life in Cherokee communities. The Cherokee have a deep respect for the natural world and are actively involved in conservation efforts. Programs focused on protecting natural resources, restoring native plant species, and promoting sustainable practices are common. Imagine a community garden where people grow vegetables, herbs, and traditional plants, fostering a connection to the land and promoting healthy living.

Education, cultural preservation, and economic development are supported by robust social services. Programs addressing housing, food security, and family support help ensure that community members have access to the resources they need. Imagine a family receiving assistance from a housing program to build a safe and comfortable home, or attending a workshop on financial literacy to improve their economic well-being. These services are designed to empower individuals and strengthen the community as a whole.

The integration of modern infrastructure with traditional values creates a unique environment in Cherokee communities. Roads, schools, healthcare facilities, and businesses are designed to meet contemporary needs while respecting cultural heritage. Imagine a modern building constructed using traditional Cherokee architectural elements, symbolizing the blend of old and new. This thoughtful integration helps maintain a strong sense of identity and continuity.

Sports and recreation are also important in Cherokee life. Many communities have facilities for basketball, baseball, and other sports, as well as opportunities for traditional games like stickball. Picture a lively game of stickball, with players demonstrating skill and teamwork, cheered on by enthusiastic spectators. These activities promote physical health, teamwork, and community spirit.

Technology and innovation are embraced in many areas, from education and healthcare to business and governance. The Cherokee Nation has developed sophisticated systems for managing resources, providing services, and communicating with members. Imagine a digital platform where community members can access information, apply for services, and connect with each other. This use of technology enhances efficiency and accessibility, helping to meet the needs of a modern community.

efforts to preserve and revive cherokee culture

One of the most significant aspects of preserving Cherokee culture is the revitalization of the Cherokee language. Imagine a classroom where children are learning to speak Cherokee, their voices enthusiastically repeating words and phrases. The language, once endangered, is being brought back to life through immersion programs and community classes. Dedicated teachers, often fluent speakers themselves, use innovative methods to make learning engaging and effective. Digital resources, such as apps and online courses, have also been developed to help people of all ages learn Cherokee at their own pace.

Efforts to preserve the language go beyond the classroom. Picture families at home, making a conscious effort to speak Cherokee during meals and daily activities. Community events, such as storytelling nights and cultural festivals, provide opportunities for people to practice and hear the language in a natural setting. By integrating Cherokee into everyday life, the community ensures that the language remains a living, breathing part of their culture.

Education plays a crucial role in cultural preservation. Schools in Cherokee communities incorporate traditional knowledge and practices into their curricula. Imagine a science lesson where students learn about local plants and their medicinal uses, or a history class that includes the rich stories of Cherokee ancestors. These lessons help students connect with their heritage and understand the significance of their cultural practices. Additionally, schools celebrate Cherokee culture through events like Heritage Day, where students participate in traditional dances, games, and crafts.

Art and craftsmanship are vital components of Cherokee culture, and efforts to preserve these skills are thriving. Picture a workshop where artisans are teaching young people the art of basket weaving, pottery, and beadwork. These crafts are not only beautiful but also carry deep cultural significance, often incorporating traditional patterns and symbols. By passing on these skills, artisans ensure that the knowledge and techniques are preserved for future generations. Art shows and craft fairs provide platforms for showcasing these works, fostering pride in cultural achievements and encouraging more people to learn these traditional arts.

Traditional music and dance are also being revived and celebrated. Imagine a community gathering where the sounds of flutes and drums fill the air, and dancers perform the intricate steps of traditional dances. Music and dance classes are offered to both children and adults, helping them learn and appreciate these important cultural expressions. Festivals and ceremonies, such as the Green Corn Ceremony, provide opportunities for the community to come together, celebrate, and keep these traditions alive.

Storytelling is another essential element of Cherokee culture. Elders play a key role in preserving and sharing traditional stories, myths, and legends. Imagine a circle of children sitting around an elder, listening intently as she tells tales of their ancestors, heroes, and the natural world. These stories are more than just entertainment; they convey important lessons and values, teaching respect for nature, bravery, and community. Efforts to record and publish these stories ensure that they are accessible to future generations, preserving the wisdom and knowledge they contain.

The Cherokee are also making strides in preserving their history and heritage through museums and cultural centers. Imagine visiting a Cherokee museum, where exhibits display artifacts, photographs, and interactive displays that tell the story of the Cherokee people. These institutions serve as repositories of history and culture, offering educational programs and resources for both the community and visitors. Cultural centers often host workshops, lectures, and events that promote a deeper understanding of Cherokee heritage and foster cultural exchange.

Community gardens and environmental programs are part of the effort to maintain traditional practices and knowledge. Imagine a garden where community members grow traditional Cherokee crops, such as corn, beans, and squash, using sustainable farming methods passed down through generations. These gardens provide not only food but also a space for learning and community building. Environmental programs focus on conservation and the protection of natural resources, reflecting the Cherokee's deep respect for the land. By involving young people in these initiatives, the community ensures that traditional ecological knowledge is preserved and applied in modern contexts.

Cultural preservation is also supported by the Cherokee Nation's government, which implements policies and programs to promote and protect cultural heritage. Imagine a council meeting where leaders discuss initiatives to support language revitalization, arts funding, and cultural education. Government grants and support enable many of the programs and activities that keep Cherokee culture vibrant and dynamic. Collaboration with other Native American tribes and organizations also helps to strengthen cultural preservation efforts and share best practices.

Technology plays an increasingly important role in preserving and sharing Cherokee culture. Imagine a virtual reality experience that allows users to explore a traditional Cherokee village or participate in a historic ceremony. Online platforms and social media provide ways to share cultural content, connect with community members, and reach a broader audience. Digital archives preserve important documents, photographs, and recordings, making them accessible to researchers and the public. By embracing technology, the Cherokee ensure that their culture remains relevant and accessible in the digital age.

The efforts to preserve and revive Cherokee culture are not just about looking back; they are about creating a vibrant and sustainable future. By honoring their heritage and adapting it to contemporary life, the Cherokee people demonstrate resilience and creativity. Imagine a future where Cherokee children grow up fluent in their language, skilled in traditional arts, and deeply connected to their history and community. This vision drives the ongoing work to preserve and celebrate

Cherokee culture, ensuring that it continues to thrive for generations to come.

As we consider these efforts, it is clear that the Cherokee people's commitment to their culture is unwavering. Their actions inspire us to value our own heritage and recognize the importance of preserving cultural diversity. The story of the Cherokee is one of resilience, creativity, and community, offering valuable lessons for us all. Through their dedication and innovation, the Cherokee continue to honor their past while building a vibrant and dynamic future.

programs to teach cherokee language and traditions

Programs to Teach Cherokee Language and Traditions

Imagine stepping into a vibrant classroom filled with eager students, their faces alight with curiosity and excitement. They are not just learning the usual subjects; they are also diving deep into the Cherokee language and traditions. The Cherokee people have developed a variety of programs to ensure that their language and cultural practices are passed down to future generations. These initiatives are essential for preserving their rich heritage and fostering a strong sense of identity and community.

One of the most significant efforts is the Cherokee Language Immersion School. Picture a group of young children, speaking and learning entirely in Cherokee from the moment they enter the classroom. The immersion program is designed to create a natural and engaging environment for language learning. Teachers, fluent in Cherokee, use songs, games, and interactive activities to make learning fun and effective. Imagine the children playing a game of "Cherokee Simon Says," following commands in Cherokee, and giggling as they learn new words and phrases.

In addition to the immersion school, there are evening and weekend classes for older students and adults. These classes cater to different proficiency levels, ensuring that everyone, from beginners to advanced speakers, can find the right fit. Imagine a classroom where adults gather after a long day, dedicated to learning their ancestral language. The teacher might lead them through conversational practice, vocabulary drills, and reading exercises, fostering a supportive and encouraging atmosphere. These classes help bridge the gap between generations, allowing grandparents and grandchildren to communicate in Cherokee and share their cultural heritage.

Technology plays a crucial role in expanding access to Cherokee language education. Imagine a family sitting around their computer, using an interactive app designed to teach Cherokee. These digital resources include vocabulary games, pronunciation guides, and cultural lessons, making it easier for people to learn at their own pace. Online courses and virtual classrooms provide flexibility, enabling people from different parts of the country to participate. Imagine joining an online class where participants from various states practice speaking Cherokee together, their faces lit up on a screen as they connect over their shared heritage.

Cultural education programs complement language learning by immersing students in traditional practices and knowledge. Imagine a summer camp where children spend their days learning about Cherokee customs, crafts, and history. They might start the day with a storytelling session, listening to an elder share tales of their ancestors. Picture the campers sitting in a circle, their eyes wide with fascination as they hear about the origins of the Cherokee people and the lessons embedded in their myths and legends. These stories not only entertain but also impart valuable cultural and moral lessons.

Hands-on activities are a vital part of these programs. Imagine children learning to weave baskets from river cane, guided by skilled artisans who explain the significance of the patterns and techniques. They might also learn to make traditional pottery, their hands shaping clay into pots and bowls that reflect centuries of Cherokee craftsmanship. These activities help students develop a deep appreciation for their heritage and the skills that have been passed down through generations.

Traditional music and dance are also integral to cultural education programs. Imagine a group of students learning to play the Cherokee flute, their fingers moving over the instrument as they produce hauntingly beautiful melodies. They might also practice traditional dances, their movements synchronized with the rhythm of drums and chants. These music and dance sessions are not just about learning techniques; they are about feeling the connection to their ancestors and expressing their cultural identity through art.

Storytelling remains a cornerstone of cultural education. Imagine an evening around a campfire, where an elder recounts the history and traditions of the Cherokee people. The flickering flames illuminate the listeners' faces as they are transported to a different time and place through the power of storytelling. These sessions provide a unique opportunity for intergenerational learning, where young people absorb the wisdom and experiences of their elders, ensuring that these stories continue to be told.

Environmental education is another critical component of these programs. Imagine a group of students hiking through a forest with a knowledgeable guide who explains the significance of different plants and animals in Cherokee culture. They might learn about traditional uses of medicinal plants, sustainable farming practices, and the importance of maintaining harmony with nature. These lessons instill a deep respect for the environment and an understanding of the interconnectedness of all living things, core values in Cherokee culture.

Cultural centers and museums play a pivotal role in preserving and teaching Cherokee traditions. Imagine visiting a cultural center where exhibits showcase Cherokee art, artifacts, and historical documents. Interactive displays allow visitors to learn about the Cherokee way of life, from traditional clothing and tools to contemporary art and music. These centers often host workshops, lectures, and cultural events, providing a space for the community to come together and celebrate their heritage.

The Cherokee Nation also supports cultural preservation through various initiatives and grants. Imagine a grant program that funds language classes, cultural workshops, and community events. These grants enable individuals and organizations to develop and expand programs that teach Cherokee language and traditions. By investing in cultural preservation, the Cherokee Nation ensures that these efforts are sustainable and impactful.

Community events and festivals provide additional opportunities for learning and celebration. Imagine a bustling festival where people of all ages gather to enjoy traditional food, music, and crafts. There might be demonstrations of traditional skills, such as pottery-making or basket-weaving, as well as performances of traditional songs and dances. These events foster a sense of community pride and unity, bringing people together to honor their shared heritage.

The success of these programs relies heavily on the dedication and passion of educators, elders, and community members. Imagine a devoted teacher who spends countless hours preparing lessons and finding new ways to engage students. Or an elder who takes the time to share their knowledge and stories, ensuring that the next generation understands the importance of their cultural heritage. These individuals are the backbone of cultural preservation efforts, their commitment inspiring others to take an active role in learning and teaching Cherokee traditions.

Sarah Michaels

role of schools and cultural centers

Imagine a typical day in a Cherokee language immersion school. From the moment students arrive, they are encouraged to speak and interact in Cherokee. Teachers use immersive techniques to help students become fluent, incorporating language learning into every aspect of the day. During a science lesson, students might learn about the different plants used in traditional medicine, naming each one in Cherokee and discussing its uses. In art class, they might create traditional beadwork or pottery, all while conversing in their native language. These immersive experiences help students develop a deep connection to their language and culture.

Cultural centers complement the work done in schools by providing a space for the broader community to come together and engage in cultural activities. Imagine walking into a cultural center where the smell of traditional Cherokee food fills the air, and the sounds of flutes and drums create a welcoming atmosphere. These centers host a variety of programs and events that cater to all ages, from storytelling sessions for young children to workshops on traditional crafts for adults. They are places where people can learn, share, and celebrate their culture.

One of the key functions of cultural centers is to serve as repositories of knowledge. They often house museums and archives that preserve important artifacts, documents, and recordings. Imagine a museum exhibit showcasing ancient pottery, tools, and ceremonial items, each with a story to tell. Interactive displays might allow visitors to hear recordings of traditional songs or watch videos of historical reenactments. These exhibits provide a tangible connection to the past and help educate visitors about the rich history of the Cherokee people.

Workshops and classes offered at cultural centers are vital for skill-building and cultural transmission. Picture a group of teenagers learning to carve traditional masks under the guidance of a skilled artisan. Each session not only teaches technical skills but also imparts the cultural significance of the craft. Similarly, language classes for adults help those who may not have had the opportunity to learn Cherokee as children. Imagine a room filled with eager learners, practicing vocabulary and pronunciation, and sharing their experiences and reasons for learning the language. These classes foster a sense of community and shared purpose.

Festivals and events held at cultural centers are vibrant celebrations of Cherokee culture. Imagine a festival day where the grounds are filled with stalls selling traditional foods, artisans demonstrating their crafts, and musicians performing traditional songs. Dance competitions, storytelling circles, and games like stickball are highlights of these events, drawing participants of all ages. These festivals are more than just entertainment; they are opportunities for cultural exchange and reinforcement of community bonds.

Schools and cultural centers also play a crucial role in the emotional and psychological well-being of the community. They provide a sense of continuity and belonging, especially for young people who are navigating their identities. Imagine a teenager participating in a youth group at a cultural center, where they can discuss their experiences, learn about their heritage, and receive support from mentors. These programs help young people build confidence and pride in their Cherokee identity, giving them a strong foundation for the future.

The role of elders in these institutions is invaluable. Elders are revered as the keepers of wisdom and tradition. Imagine an elder sitting in a circle of children, telling stories of their ancestors and imparting lessons about respect, bravery, and community. Their presence in schools and cultural centers bridges the gap between generations, ensuring that traditional knowledge is not lost. Elders often lead ceremonies and rituals, providing spiritual guidance and reinforcing cultural values.

Technology is increasingly being used in schools and cultural centers to enhance learning and preservation efforts. Imagine a digital archive where students can access recordings of traditional songs, oral histories, and instructional videos on crafts and ceremonies. Virtual reality experiences might allow visitors to explore a traditional Cherokee village or participate in a historic event. These technological tools make cultural education more accessible and engaging, especially for younger generations who are adept at using digital platforms.

Partnerships with other educational and cultural institutions also enrich the programs offered by Cherokee schools and cultural centers. Collaborations with universities, museums, and cultural organizations can provide additional resources and expertise. Imagine a university linguistics department working with a Cherokee school to develop advanced language learning materials, or a national museum hosting a traveling exhibit of Cherokee artifacts. These partnerships help broaden the reach and impact of cultural preservation efforts.

Community involvement is essential to the success of these institutions. Parents, grandparents, and other community members often volunteer their time and skills to support programs and events. Imagine a parent leading a weekend workshop on traditional cooking, or a group of community members organizing a fundraising event to support the school. This collective effort ensures that cultural education is a shared responsibility and that everyone has a stake in preserving their heritage.

8 / cherokee contributions and notable figures

profiles of notable cherokee leaders

SEQUOYAH: The Creator of the Cherokee Syllabary

Picture a dedicated silversmith named Sequoyah, who noticed that European settlers used written symbols to communicate. Fascinated by this concept, he set out to create a written language for the Cherokee. Despite skepticism and resistance from some of his people, Sequoyah was determined. Imagine him painstakingly developing each character, ensuring it could be easily learned and used.

Sequoyah's efforts resulted in the Cherokee syllabary, a set of written symbols that represent syllables rather than individual letters. This innovation allowed the Cherokee to develop a written language that was both practical and efficient. Imagine the excitement and pride within the Cherokee community as they began to read and write in their own language. The syllabary enabled the publication of books, newspapers, and legal documents, significantly enhancing communication and literacy among the Cherokee.

. . .

Sarah Michaels

Sequoyah's contribution extended beyond the realm of language. His work empowered the Cherokee people, providing them with a tool to preserve their culture and history. Today, his legacy is celebrated, and his syllabary remains a cornerstone of Cherokee cultural preservation.

Chief John Ross: The Resilient Leader

John Ross, known as Tsan-Usdi to the Cherokee, was a leader whose life was marked by his dedication to his people during one of the most challenging periods in their history. Imagine Ross, a young man of mixed Scottish and Cherokee heritage, rising to prominence due to his intelligence, diplomatic skills, and commitment to his community.

As Principal Chief, Ross tirelessly advocated for the rights of the Cherokee Nation. His leadership was crucial during the time of the Indian Removal Act and the Trail of Tears. Imagine Ross traveling to Washington, D.C., multiple times to negotiate with the U.S. government, presenting petitions, and seeking legal recourse to protect Cherokee lands. Despite his efforts, the Treaty of New Echota was signed by a minority faction, leading to the forced relocation of the Cherokee people.

Ross's resilience shone through during the Trail of Tears. He led his people through the ordeal, offering guidance and support. Imagine him walking alongside his fellow Cherokee, sharing in their suffering and striving to maintain their spirit and unity. After the relocation, Ross worked to rebuild the Cherokee Nation in Indian Territory, helping to establish a new government and community structures.

. . .

John Ross's legacy is one of unwavering commitment and leadership. His efforts helped the Cherokee Nation survive one of its darkest chapters and laid the groundwork for its recovery and future growth.

Wilma Mankiller: The First Female Principal Chief

Wilma Mankiller's story is one of breaking barriers and inspiring change. Imagine a young Wilma growing up in a poor, rural community, facing numerous challenges yet determined to make a difference. Her path led her to activism and leadership, where she became a powerful advocate for the Cherokee people.

In 1985, Mankiller was elected as the first female Principal Chief of the Cherokee Nation. Her election was a significant milestone, symbolizing progress and the empowerment of women within the community. Imagine Mankiller stepping into her role with a vision for revitalizing the Cherokee Nation. She focused on improving healthcare, education, and economic opportunities for her people.

Under her leadership, the Cherokee Nation saw significant advancements. Mankiller promoted self-sufficiency and community development projects, empowering local communities to take control of their futures. Imagine her working alongside community members, developing housing projects, creating jobs, and improving access to healthcare services.

Wilma Mankiller's legacy is one of transformation and empowerment. Her leadership demonstrated the strength and potential of the Cherokee Nation, inspiring future generations to continue building on her achievements.

Sarah Michaels

. . .

Charles "Chief" Harris: The Cultural Guardian

Charles "Chief" Harris is known for his dedication to preserving and promoting Cherokee culture. Imagine a young Harris, deeply immersed in Cherokee traditions, learning the language, stories, and customs from his elders. His passion for his heritage led him to become a respected cultural ambassador and educator.

Harris's contributions include the establishment of cultural programs and initiatives aimed at teaching Cherokee traditions to younger generations. Imagine Harris leading a workshop on traditional Cherokee crafts, his hands deftly weaving baskets while sharing stories and teachings. His efforts have helped ensure that vital cultural practices are passed down and remain vibrant.

As a storyteller, Harris has brought Cherokee legends and history to life. Picture him at a community gathering, captivating his audience with tales of ancient heroes, tricksters, and creation myths. Through his storytelling, Harris preserves the oral traditions that are central to Cherokee identity and culture.

Charles Harris's legacy is one of cultural preservation and education. His work ensures that the rich heritage of the Cherokee people continues to thrive and be cherished by future generations.

Chad "Corntassel" Smith: The Modernizer

Chad "Corntassel" Smith, who served as Principal Chief

from 1999 to 2011, played a pivotal role in modernizing the Cherokee Nation. Imagine Smith, a visionary leader, taking office with a commitment to bringing the Cherokee Nation into the 21st century while honoring its traditions.

Under Smith's leadership, the Cherokee Nation experienced significant economic growth and development. He focused on education, healthcare, and infrastructure, implementing programs that improved the quality of life for the Cherokee people. Imagine new schools being built, healthcare facilities being upgraded, and economic initiatives creating job opportunities and fostering entrepreneurship.

Smith also prioritized the preservation of Cherokee language and culture. Imagine him supporting language immersion programs and cultural events that celebrate Cherokee heritage. His leadership helped bridge the gap between modern advancements and traditional values, ensuring that progress did not come at the expense of cultural identity.

Chad Smith's legacy is one of innovation and progress. His efforts have strengthened the Cherokee Nation, making it more resilient and better equipped to face future challenges.

achievements of cherokee individuals in various fields

Medicine and Science: Dr. Adrienne Stith Butler

Imagine a young girl, fascinated by the workings of the human body, determined to make a difference in the field of medicine. This girl grew up to be Dr. Adrienne Stith Butler, a renowned psychologist and researcher. Picture Dr. Butler in her lab, conducting groundbreaking research that addresses critical health disparities. Her work focuses on mental health, substance abuse, and the social determinants of health, aiming to improve the well-being of marginalized communities.

Dr. Butler's contributions extend beyond research. She is a respected author and speaker, advocating for policies that promote health equity. Imagine her speaking at a conference, sharing insights that influence public health strategies and inspire new generations of healthcare professionals. Her achievements highlight the importance of addressing mental health and social issues, reinforcing the Cherokee values of community and care.

Literature and Education: Joy Harjo

Picture a poet whose words capture the essence of Cherokee culture, weaving together stories of resilience, nature, and history. Joy Harjo, the first Native American Poet Laureate of the United States, uses her poetry to celebrate her heritage and address social injustices. Imagine Harjo at a poetry reading, her voice resonating with audiences as she brings to life the experiences and dreams of her people.

Harjo's influence extends to education as well. She is a passionate advocate for incorporating Native American literature and history into school curricula. Picture her visiting a classroom, engaging with students and inspiring them to explore their own cultural identities through writing. Her work as a poet, musician, and educator underscores the power of the arts to foster understanding and cultural appreciation.

Sports: Jim Thorpe

Imagine the roar of the crowd as Jim Thorpe, one of the

greatest athletes of all time, takes the field. Thorpe, of Sac and Fox and Cherokee descent, excelled in multiple sports, including football, baseball, and track and field. Picture Thorpe competing in the 1912 Stockholm Olympics, where he won gold medals in the pentathlon and decathlon, showcasing his extraordinary athleticism and versatility.

Thorpe's legacy goes beyond his athletic achievements. He became an advocate for Native American rights and worked to promote sports as a means of empowerment for young people. Imagine a young athlete looking up to Thorpe, inspired by his determination and success. Thorpe's story is a testament to the strength and potential within the Cherokee community and the impact one individual can have on the world.

Business and Entrepreneurship: Chad "Corntassel" Smith

Envision a leader who transformed the economic landscape of the Cherokee Nation. Chad "Corntassel" Smith, who served as Principal Chief from 1999 to 2011, implemented policies that spurred economic growth and development. Picture Smith at a groundbreaking ceremony for a new business venture, emphasizing the importance of self-sufficiency and economic independence for the Cherokee people.

Smith's initiatives included the establishment of Cherokee Nation Businesses, which created jobs and generated revenue for the community. Imagine a thriving business environment where Cherokee entrepreneurs innovate and succeed, supported by the frameworks Smith helped to establish. His achievements in business and governance demonstrate the power of visionary leadership and its lasting impact on the community.

. . .

Sarah Michaels

Technology: John Herrington

Imagine a young boy gazing at the stars, dreaming of exploring space. This boy grew up to be John Herrington, the first Native American astronaut. Picture Herrington aboard the Space Shuttle Endeavour, conducting scientific experiments and spacewalks. His journey to space symbolizes the limitless possibilities for Cherokee individuals and serves as an inspiration to aspiring scientists and engineers.

Herrington's contributions to science and technology extend beyond his space missions. He is dedicated to promoting STEM (Science, Technology, Engineering, and Mathematics) education among Native American youth. Imagine Herrington speaking at a school, sharing his experiences and encouraging students to pursue careers in science and technology. His achievements highlight the importance of representation and the potential for innovation within the Cherokee community.

Law and Justice: Mary Golda Ross

Envision a trailblazing woman who broke barriers in the field of aerospace engineering. Mary Golda Ross, the first known Native American female engineer, made significant contributions to the development of space travel and missile technology. Picture Ross working on classified projects for NASA and Lockheed Martin, her expertise and innovation driving advancements in aerospace technology.

Ross's legacy extends to her advocacy for education and career opportunities for Native American women in STEM fields. Imagine a scholarship program established in her name, supporting young women who aspire to follow in her footsteps. Ross's achievements in engineering and her commitment to mentorship and advocacy reflect the values of knowledge and community service that are central to Cherokee culture.

Music and Arts: Jimi Hendrix
Imagine the electrifying sound of a guitar that changed the landscape of rock music. Jimi Hendrix, of Cherokee descent through his grandmother, revolutionized the music world with his innovative guitar techniques and iconic performances. Picture Hendrix on stage at Woodstock, captivating the audience with his unparalleled talent and creativity.

Hendrix's influence extends beyond his music. He is celebrated for his contributions to the arts and his role in breaking down racial barriers in the entertainment industry. Imagine young musicians inspired by Hendrix, picking up their guitars and experimenting with new sounds. His legacy in music and his impact on popular culture underscore the importance of artistic expression and innovation within the Cherokee community.

9 / activities and projects

crafts

BASKET MAKING: Weaving Stories with Willow

Basket making is a cherished craft among the Cherokee, passed down through generations. Imagine sitting around a table with your family, ready to create your first simple basket. The process starts with gathering the materials. Traditionally, Cherokee baskets are made from river cane, white oak, or honeysuckle. For our simple basket, we'll use willow, a material that is flexible and easy to work with.

First, let's prepare the willow. Imagine soaking the willow strips in water to make them pliable. This step is essential, as it allows the willow to bend without breaking. As you soak the strips, you can think about the countless generations before you who have performed this same task, preparing materials with care and respect.

Once the willow is ready, we start with the base. Picture laying out eight strips of willow in a crisscross pattern, four hori-

Sarah Michaels

zontal and four vertical. These strips form the framework of your basket. Now, take another strip of willow and begin weaving it over and under the framework strips, securing them together. This initial weaving is called the "God's eye" and provides a sturdy base for your basket.

With the base complete, it's time to build the sides. Imagine picking up another strip of willow and continuing the over-and-under weaving pattern, but this time working your way around the base. As you weave, the basket begins to take shape, each row adding height and structure. Pay attention to the tension in the willow strips; they should be snug but not too tight, allowing the basket to maintain its shape while remaining flexible.

As you continue weaving, you might notice how meditative the process can be. Each movement, each strip woven into place, becomes a rhythm. This repetitive action allows your mind to wander, perhaps imagining the stories and uses for your basket. Will it hold fresh berries from a summer's day picking? Or perhaps it will carry wildflowers collected on a nature walk?

Once you've reached the desired height, it's time to finish the rim. Imagine folding the ends of the willow strips over the top edge and weaving them back into the basket to secure the rim. This step ensures that the basket is sturdy and that the edges are smooth and neat.

Finally, admire your work. The simple basket you've created is not just a functional object; it's a piece of your heritage, woven with stories and traditions. Each basket is unique, reflecting the hands that made it and the care taken in its creation.

Beadwork: Crafting Patterns and History

Now, let's explore beadwork, another beloved Cherokee craft. Imagine a table covered with tiny, colorful beads, each one a potential part of a beautiful pattern. Beadwork is often used to create intricate designs on clothing, accessories, and ceremonial items, each pattern telling a story or representing a symbol.

To begin, gather your materials: a needle, thread, and beads. For a simple project, let's create a beaded bracelet. Imagine threading the needle and tying a knot at the end of the thread, ready to start your design.

First, decide on a pattern. Traditional Cherokee beadwork often features geometric designs, inspired by nature and symbolic meanings. Imagine sketching a simple pattern on a piece of paper, perhaps a zigzag or diamond shape, which you'll replicate with your beads.

Start by threading the first bead onto the needle and pushing it down to the knot at the end of the thread. Continue adding beads according to your pattern, threading them one by one. Picture the beads coming together, each one adding to the emerging design. The rhythm of threading beads, similar to weaving, becomes a soothing, repetitive action.

As you work, consider the significance of the colors and patterns you're using. In Cherokee culture, different colors can

Sarah Michaels

symbolize various elements of nature and spiritual beliefs. For example, red might represent success and triumph, while blue could symbolize peace and harmony. Imagine choosing colors that resonate with you and the story you want your bracelet to tell.

Once you've completed your pattern, it's time to finish the bracelet. Imagine tying off the end of the thread securely and trimming any excess. If you're making a bracelet, you might add a clasp or simply tie the ends together to fit your wrist.

Admire your creation. Each bead in your bracelet is a small piece of a larger story, a reflection of Cherokee traditions and your personal creativity. Beadwork, like basket-making, is a craft that connects you to your heritage, allowing you to carry a piece of your culture with you.

Both basket making and beadwork are more than just crafts; they are expressions of Cherokee identity and history. These activities provide a way to preserve and celebrate cultural traditions, passing them down through generations. As you weave a basket or thread beads into a pattern, you are participating in a continuum of creativity and storytelling that has been part of Cherokee life for centuries.

Imagine sharing these crafts with others, teaching a friend or family member how to make their own basket or beaded bracelet. Each lesson is an opportunity to pass on knowledge and keep traditions alive. These shared experiences foster a sense of community and connection, strengthening the bonds between individuals and their heritage.

· · ·

By engaging in these crafts, you not only create beautiful objects but also become part of a larger narrative. You honor the skills and artistry of those who came before you, ensuring that their legacy continues to inspire and enrich the lives of future generations. Whether through the simple act of weaving a basket or the intricate process of beading, you contribute to the vibrant tapestry of Cherokee culture, preserving its beauty and significance for years to come.

cooking traditional cherokee recipes

Bean Bread (Tsu-Ya-Ga-Di)

Let's start with a beloved Cherokee recipe: bean bread, or Tsu-Ya-Ga-Di. This dish is a staple in Cherokee cuisine, known for its simplicity and heartiness. Imagine gathering around the table with your family, ready to make this delicious bread.

Begin by gathering your ingredients: dried corn kernels, dried beans (such as pinto or kidney beans), salt, and water. Picture yourself rinsing the beans and corn thoroughly, preparing them for cooking. Soak the corn overnight to soften it, which will make it easier to grind.

The next day, imagine draining the soaked corn and grinding it into a coarse meal. This step can be done using a traditional stone grinder or a modern food processor. As you grind the corn, think about the generations of Cherokee who have performed this same task, their hands turning the stones and transforming the corn into meal.

Now, place the beans in a pot of water and bring them to a boil. Cook the beans until they are tender, then drain and mash them lightly with a fork. Combine the mashed beans with the cornmeal, adding a pinch of salt to taste. Mix the ingredients together until they form a dough-like consistency.

Next, imagine shaping the dough into small, round loaves. Place the loaves in a pot of boiling water, ensuring they are fully submerged. Cover the pot and let the bread cook for about an hour, until the loaves are firm and fully cooked through. As they cook, the kitchen fills with the comforting aroma of bean bread, evoking memories of family gatherings and cultural celebrations.

Once the bread is done, carefully remove it from the pot and let it cool slightly. Imagine breaking open a loaf of bean bread, the steam rising as you reveal the soft, flavorful interior. Serve the bread warm, perhaps with a drizzle of honey or a pat of butter, and enjoy the simple, satisfying taste of this traditional dish.

Kanuchi (Hickory Nut Soup)

Next, let's make Kanuchi, a rich and flavorful hickory nut soup that is a true delight. Imagine gathering hickory nuts, cracking their hard shells, and extracting the meat inside. This process requires patience and care, but the effort is well worth it.

To prepare the Kanuchi, start by roasting the hickory nuts to bring out their natural oils and enhance their flavor. Imagine the nuts turning a golden brown in the oven, filling the kitchen with their rich, nutty aroma. Once roasted, grind the nuts into a fine paste using a mortar and pestle or a food processor.

· · ·

In a large pot, bring water to a boil. Gradually stir in the hickory nut paste, mixing until it is fully dissolved in the water. Imagine the soup thickening as it simmers, the nutty aroma intensifying. Add a pinch of salt to enhance the flavor, and let the soup cook until it reaches a creamy, smooth consistency.

Kanuchi is often served with cornmeal dumplings or bread. Imagine dropping small spoonfuls of cornmeal dough into the simmering soup, watching as they puff up and cook through. The combination of the rich, creamy soup and the tender dumplings creates a comforting and nourishing dish.

Ladle the Kanuchi into bowls and enjoy it hot. The warm, nutty flavor is both satisfying and nourishing, a true taste of Cherokee culinary tradition.

Fried Hominy (Bigu-Ni)

Fried hominy, or Bigu-Ni, is another cherished Cherokee dish. Imagine starting with dried hominy corn, soaking it overnight to rehydrate the kernels. Once soaked, rinse the hominy thoroughly and drain it.

In a large skillet, heat some oil over medium heat. Add the drained hominy to the skillet, spreading it out in an even layer. Imagine the kernels sizzling as they hit the hot oil, their edges beginning to brown and crisp. Stir the hominy occasionally, allowing it to cook evenly and develop a golden-brown color.

As the hominy fries, season it with a pinch of salt and pepper. For a bit of extra flavor, you might add some diced onions or bell peppers, sautéing them alongside the hominy until they are tender and fragrant. The combination of crispy hominy and sautéed vegetables creates a delightful texture and flavor.

Serve the fried hominy hot, as a side dish or a snack. Its crunchy exterior and tender interior make it a satisfying treat, perfect for sharing with family and friends.

Cherokee Grape Dumplings (A-Ni-Wa-Ya)

For a sweet treat, let's make Cherokee grape dumplings, or A-Ni-Wa-Ya. This dessert is a favorite at Cherokee gatherings, combining the tartness of grapes with the comforting taste of homemade dumplings.

Begin by preparing a grape sauce. Imagine simmering fresh or frozen grapes in a pot with a bit of water, allowing the fruit to break down and release its juices. Once the grapes are soft, strain the mixture through a sieve to remove the seeds and skins, leaving a smooth, flavorful grape sauce.

In a mixing bowl, combine flour, baking powder, and a pinch of salt. Add water gradually, mixing until you form a smooth dough. Imagine rolling out the dough on a floured surface, then cutting it into small squares or strips.

Bring the grape sauce back to a simmer and gently drop the dough pieces into the pot. Imagine the dumplings cooking in the sweet grape sauce, absorbing the flavor and becoming tender. Let the dumplings simmer until they are fully cooked, stirring occasionally to prevent sticking.

· · ·

Serve the grape dumplings warm, perhaps with a drizzle of honey or a sprinkle of sugar. The combination of sweet grape sauce and soft, pillowy dumplings is a delightful end to any meal, evoking the flavors and traditions of Cherokee cuisine.

Cooking traditional Cherokee recipes is more than just preparing food; it's a way to connect with heritage, share stories, and celebrate culture. Each dish carries with it the history and traditions of the Cherokee people, passed down through generations. By making these recipes, you are preserving and honoring that legacy, bringing the rich flavors and vibrant traditions of Cherokee cuisine into your home.

basic cherokee words and phrases

Greetings and Introductions

Let's start with some simple greetings. Imagine meeting a Cherokee friend and wanting to greet them warmly. Here's how you can say "hello":

Osiyo (oh-see-yo) – Hello

This is the most common way to say hello in Cherokee. Picture yourself greeting someone with a friendly "Osiyo," and seeing their face light up with recognition and warmth.

When introducing yourself, you might want to say your name. Here's how you can do that:

. . .

Sarah Michaels

Dagwado (dah-gwah-doh) – My name is...

To introduce yourself, say "Dagwado" followed by your name. For example, if your name is John, you would say, "Dagwado John." Imagine meeting new people and confidently sharing your name in Cherokee.

If you want to ask someone else's name, you can say:

Gado hadvne (gah-doh hah-duh-nay) – What is your name?
   Common Phrases
   Wado (wah-doh) – Thank you

This simple word carries a lot of gratitude. Picture yourself expressing thanks with a heartfelt "Wado," making your appreciation clear and genuine.

If someone thanks you and you want to say "you're welcome," use this phrase:

Tla (tlah) – No (also used as "You're welcome" in response to thanks)

Imagine the ease of responding to gratitude with a polite "Tla," showing your understanding and respect for the language.

If you need to apologize or say "I'm sorry," you can use:

· · ·

Sga-du (s-gah-doo) – I'm sorry

This phrase is useful in many situations. Picture yourself making a small mistake and then gracefully saying "Sga-du" to acknowledge it.

Numbers and Counting
   1. Saquu (sah-koo)
   2. Tali (tah-lee)
   3. Tsoi (tso-ee)
   4. Nvhgi (nuh-gee)
   5. Hisgi (hees-gee)
   6. Sudali (soo-dah-lee)
   7. Galiquogi (gah-lee-kwoh-gee)
   8. Tsaneli (tsah-nay-lee)
   9. Sone (so-nay)
   10. Sgoi (s-goh-ee)

Basic Conversation
Tohiquu (toh-hee-koo) – How are you?

This question shows you care about the other person's well-being. Picture the friendly interactions you can have when you ask someone "Tohiquu."

To respond to this question, you can say:

Tohi (toh-hee) – I'm fine

Imagine someone asking you how you are, and you respond with a calm "Tohi," letting them know you're doing well.

Sarah Michaels

• • •

If you want to tell someone that something is good, you can use:

Osda (oh-s-dah) – Good

This word is versatile and can be used in many contexts. Picture yourself using "Osda" to compliment someone's cooking or to agree that something is enjoyable.

When you want to express understanding, you can say:

Hia (hee-ah) – Yes

This word is simple but powerful. Imagine using "Hia" in a conversation to show that you agree or understand what someone is saying.

If you need to say no or disagree, use:

Tla (tlah) – No

Practical Phrases
    Hagata (hah-gah-tah) – Where is...?

• • •

This phrase can help you navigate new places or find things you need. Picture yourself asking, "Hagata?" and then following with the name of what you're looking for.

If you need to ask for help, you can say:

Ayoli (ah-yo-lee) – Help

Imagine finding yourself in a situation where you need assistance. Saying "Ayoli" can quickly get someone's attention and help you out.

When you're saying goodbye, you can use:

Donadagohvi (doe-nah-dah-go-huh-vee) – Until we meet again (a more formal way to say goodbye)

This phrase carries a sense of optimism and the promise of seeing each other again. Picture yourself parting ways with a friend and using "Donadagohvi" to wish them well until your next meeting.

Incorporating Cherokee into Daily Life

Consider labeling common household items with their Cherokee names. This practice can help reinforce your vocabulary and make learning more interactive. Imagine seeing a label on your door that says "noquisi" (door), or a label on your table that says "gawoni" (table), reminding you of the Cherokee word every time you see it.

Sarah Michaels

· · ·

You can also practice Cherokee with friends and family. Imagine having a family dinner where you all try to use as many Cherokee words and phrases as possible. This shared learning experience can be fun and educational, strengthening both your language skills and your bonds with each other.

Language learning is a journey, and every word and phrase you learn is a step toward preserving and celebrating Cherokee culture. By incorporating these basic Cherokee words and phrases into your conversations, you are contributing to the vitality of the language and keeping its spirit alive for future generations.

glosary

Cherokee (Tsalagi)

The term "Cherokee" refers to the Native American people originally from the southeastern United States. The Cherokee call themselves "Tsalagi" in their own language. Imagine a community of people with a rich history, vibrant culture, and enduring spirit, known for their resilience and contributions to society. Understanding the term "Cherokee" connects you to a group whose history spans centuries and whose influence continues today.

Syllabary

A syllabary is a set of written symbols that represent syllables, which make up words. The Cherokee syllabary was created by Sequoyah in the early 19th century, revolutionizing literacy for the Cherokee people. Picture a chart filled with unique symbols, each representing a sound in the Cherokee language. This innovation allowed the Cherokee to read and write in their own language, preserving their stories, laws, and traditions in written form.

Wattle and Daub

Wattle and daub is a traditional method of building homes used by the Cherokee and many other cultures around the world. Imagine a sturdy structure made from a woven lattice of wooden strips (wattle) coated with a mixture of clay, mud, and straw (daub). These homes were well-suited to the Cherokee environment, providing insulation and protection from the elements.

Clan System

The Cherokee clan system is a social structure that organizes the community into extended family groups. There are seven clans: Bird, Deer, Wolf, Blue, Long Hair, Paint, and Wild Potato. Imagine a family tree that extends far beyond immediate relatives, connecting individuals through shared ancestry and responsibilities. Each clan has its own roles, traditions, and significance within the Cherokee Nation.

Stickball (Anejo-di)

Stickball is a traditional Cherokee game similar to lacrosse, played with sticks and a small ball. The game was historically used to settle disputes and train warriors. Picture two teams on a field, each player skillfully using their sticks to catch, carry, and throw the ball, aiming to hit a target. The game is not only a sport but also a way to bring the community together and maintain physical and mental agility.

Kanuchi

Kanuchi is a traditional Cherokee soup made from hickory nuts. Imagine a warm, creamy soup with a rich, nutty flavor, often enjoyed during special gatherings and ceremonies. The process of making Kanuchi involves roasting and grinding the nuts, then cooking them into a smooth broth. This dish reflects the Cherokee's deep connection to their natural environment and their skill in utilizing available resources.

Bean Bread (Tsu-Ya-Ga-Di)

Bean bread, or Tsu-Ya-Ga-Di, is a staple in Cherokee cuisine, made from cornmeal and beans. Picture a hearty, nutritious loaf of bread, its aroma filling the kitchen as it cooks. The preparation involves soaking and grinding corn, cooking and mashing beans, and combining these ingredients to form dough that is then boiled. This traditional recipe showcases the resourcefulness and culinary heritage of the Cherokee people.

Osiyo

Osiyo means "hello" in Cherokee. Imagine greeting a friend with a warm smile and an "Osiyo," instantly connecting through a shared cultural expression. This simple word opens the door to conversation and friendship, reflecting the Cherokee values of community and hospitality.

Wado

Wado means "thank you" in Cherokee. Picture expressing your gratitude with a heartfelt "Wado," showing appreciation for kindness and assistance. This word encapsulates the importance of gratitude in Cherokee culture, fostering positive relationships and mutual respect.

Medicine Men and Women

Medicine men and women in Cherokee culture are healers who use traditional knowledge, herbal medicine, and spiritual practices to treat physical and mental ailments. Imagine a wise elder mixing herbs and conducting ceremonies to restore balance and health. These practitioners hold a revered place in Cherokee society, bridging the physical and spiritual worlds to promote well-being.

Green Corn Ceremony

The Green Corn Ceremony is a traditional Cherokee festival celebrating the first harvest of corn. Picture a vibrant gathering with dancing, feasting, and rituals to give thanks for the harvest and cleanse the community. This ceremony reflects the Cherokee's agricultural roots and their gratitude for the bounty of the earth.

Trail of Tears

The Trail of Tears refers to the forced relocation of the Cherokee people from their ancestral lands to present-day Oklahoma during the 1830s. Imagine the hardship and suffering endured by thousands as they were uprooted and made to walk hundreds of miles under harsh conditions. This

Glosary

tragic event is a pivotal moment in Cherokee history, symbolizing their resilience and determination to survive and rebuild.

Principal Chief

The Principal Chief is the highest elected official in the Cherokee Nation, responsible for leading the government and representing the people. Imagine a leader working tirelessly to advocate for the rights and well-being of their community, balancing traditional values with modern governance. The Principal Chief plays a crucial role in guiding the Cherokee Nation through challenges and opportunities.

Sequoyah

Sequoyah was a Cherokee silversmith and inventor of the Cherokee syllabary. Picture a determined individual, deeply committed to creating a writing system that would enable his people to achieve literacy. Sequoyah's invention transformed Cherokee society, empowering the community to document their language, laws, and culture in writing.

Corn, Beans, and Squash (Three Sisters)

Corn, beans, and squash, known as the Three Sisters, are central to Cherokee agriculture. Imagine fields where these three crops grow together, each supporting the others in a harmonious relationship. Corn provides a structure for beans to climb, beans add nitrogen to the soil, and squash covers the ground, preventing weeds and retaining moisture. This sustainable farming practice reflects the Cherokee's deep understanding of the natural world.

Long Hair Clan (Ani-Gilohi)

The Long Hair Clan, or Ani-Gilohi, is one of the seven Cherokee clans, traditionally known for their roles as peacekeepers and diplomats. Picture a group of individuals who are skilled in negotiation and maintaining harmony within the community. Members of the Long Hair Clan often serve as mediators and are respected for their wisdom and ability to resolve conflicts.

Beadwork

Beadwork is a traditional Cherokee craft that involves

creating intricate patterns using beads. Imagine a skilled artisan carefully stitching beads into beautiful designs that adorn clothing, accessories, and ceremonial items. Each pattern tells a story or symbolizes important cultural themes, reflecting the creativity and heritage of the Cherokee people.

Cherokee National Holiday

The Cherokee National Holiday is an annual celebration commemorating the signing of the Cherokee Constitution in 1839. Picture a lively festival with parades, traditional dances, music, arts and crafts, and community gatherings. This event honors Cherokee sovereignty and cultural heritage, bringing people together to celebrate their shared history and achievements.

Understanding these key terms helps you appreciate the depth and richness of Cherokee culture. Each word and concept opens a window into the lives, values, and traditions of the Cherokee people. As you continue to learn and explore, these terms will serve as a foundation for deeper understanding and connection to this vibrant heritage.

resources

Websites for Learning

1. Cherokee Nation Official Website (www.cherokee.org)

Imagine accessing a comprehensive resource that provides information on all aspects of Cherokee life. The official website of the Cherokee Nation includes sections on history, culture, government, and current events. It's an invaluable tool for staying informed about contemporary Cherokee issues and initiatives.

2. Cherokee Heritage Center (www.cherokeeheritage.org)

Picture a virtual visit to a museum dedicated to preserving and promoting Cherokee culture. The Cherokee Heritage Center's website offers information about exhibits, educational programs, and cultural events. It's a great starting point for anyone interested in exploring Cherokee heritage in depth.

3. Sequoyah National Research Center (ualr.edu/sequoyah)

Imagine a research center that houses a vast collection of Native American materials, including documents, photographs, and artifacts. The Sequoyah National Research Center's website provides access to these resources,

Resources

supporting research and education about Native American history and culture. It's an excellent site for those conducting in-depth studies.

4. National Museum of the American Indian (americanindian.si.edu)

Envision a museum that celebrates the diverse cultures of Native Americans, including the Cherokee. The National Museum of the American Indian's website features virtual exhibits, educational resources, and information about their extensive collections. It's a valuable resource for exploring the broader context of Native American history and culture.

5. Cherokee Phoenix (www.cherokeephoenix.org)

Picture reading a newspaper that has been serving the Cherokee Nation since 1828. The Cherokee Phoenix provides news, features, and commentary on issues affecting the Cherokee people. Its website is a great way to stay updated on current events and perspectives within the Cherokee community.

Museums to Visit

1. Cherokee Heritage Center, Tahlequah, Oklahoma

Imagine walking through exhibits that showcase the history, art, and culture of the Cherokee Nation. The Cherokee Heritage Center offers interactive displays, historical reenactments, and educational programs. Visiting this museum provides a firsthand experience of Cherokee heritage and traditions.

2. Museum of the Cherokee Indian, Cherokee, North Carolina

Picture exploring a museum dedicated to preserving and interpreting Cherokee history and culture. The Museum of the Cherokee Indian features artifacts, exhibits, and multimedia presentations that bring Cherokee stories to life. It's a must-visit destination for anyone interested in learning more about the Cherokee people.

3. National Museum of the American Indian, Washington, D.C.

Imagine a museum that represents the rich diversity of Native American cultures across the Americas. The National Museum of the American Indian includes extensive exhibits on the Cherokee and other Native American tribes. Its location in the nation's capital makes it a significant place for learning and reflection.

4. Sequoyah Birthplace Museum, Vonore, Tennessee

Picture visiting the birthplace of Sequoyah, the creator of the Cherokee syllabary. The Sequoyah Birthplace Museum offers exhibits on Sequoyah's life and legacy, as well as Cherokee history and culture. It's a unique destination that honors one of the most influential figures in Cherokee history.

5. Chieftains Museum/Major Ridge Home, Rome, Georgia

Imagine exploring the home of Major Ridge, a prominent Cherokee leader. The Chieftains Museum offers insights into the life and times of Major Ridge, as well as the broader history of the Cherokee Nation. Visiting this historic site provides a personal connection to important events and figures in Cherokee history.

appendix

timeline of significant events in cherokee history

Early History: Pre-Contact and Early European Encounters

Before 1500s: Ancient Civilization
   Picture a thriving civilization in the southeastern United States, with well-organized villages, sophisticated agricultural practices, and rich cultural traditions. The Cherokee, part of the Iroquoian language group, were known for their intricate social structures, mound-building, and trade networks that spanned vast distances.

1540: Encounter with Hernando de Soto
   Imagine the first contact between the Cherokee and Europeans when Spanish explorer Hernando de Soto ventured into their territory. This encounter marked the beginning of profound changes, as the Cherokee were introduced to new goods, diseases, and challenges brought by the Europeans.

1700s: Alliances and Conflicts

Appendix

1715-1755: Cherokee-British Alliance

Visualize a period of strategic alliances where the Cherokee allied with the British during various colonial conflicts, including the Yamasee War and the French and Indian War. These alliances were crucial for trade and military support, although they also brought complications and shifting loyalties.

1758: Fort Loudoun

Picture the construction of Fort Loudoun in present-day Tennessee, a British fortification established to strengthen alliances with the Cherokee. The fort became a focal point of cooperation and conflict, ultimately leading to its siege by the Cherokee in 1760 after deteriorating relations.

1776: Cherokee-American Conflicts

Imagine the turbulence of the American Revolutionary War reaching Cherokee lands. The Cherokee initially sided with the British, leading to clashes with American settlers and soldiers. The resulting military campaigns against the Cherokee devastated their villages and disrupted their society.

Early 1800s: Sovereignty and Displacement

1808: Cherokee Constitution

Visualize the Cherokee Nation adopting their first written constitution, establishing a centralized government modeled after the United States. This constitution was a significant step towards unifying the Cherokee under a single political framework and asserting their sovereignty.

1821: Sequoyah and the Cherokee Syllabary

Picture Sequoyah presenting the Cherokee syllabary, a revolutionary writing system that enabled widespread literacy among the Cherokee. This achievement empowered the

Cherokee to publish books, newspapers, and official documents in their own language, strengthening their cultural identity.

1830: Indian Removal Act

Imagine the tension and fear as the U.S. Congress passed the Indian Removal Act, authorizing the forced relocation of Native American tribes from their ancestral lands. This policy set the stage for one of the most tragic events in Cherokee history.

1835: Treaty of New Echota

Visualize the controversial signing of the Treaty of New Echota by a small faction of Cherokee leaders, ceding all Cherokee lands east of the Mississippi River to the United States. Despite opposition from Principal Chief John Ross and the majority of the Cherokee people, the treaty was ratified, sealing their fate.

1838-1839: Trail of Tears

Imagine the heart-wrenching journey of thousands of Cherokee as they were forcibly removed from their homes and marched to Indian Territory (present-day Oklahoma). Known as the Trail of Tears, this brutal relocation resulted in the deaths of an estimated 4,000 Cherokee due to disease, exposure, and exhaustion.

Late 1800s: Reconstruction and Adaptation

1861-1865: Civil War

Picture the Cherokee Nation divided as the American Civil War erupted. Some Cherokee sided with the Confederacy, while others supported the Union. This internal conflict further strained the community, leading to battles and significant upheaval within the Cherokee Nation.

Appendix

1866: Reconstruction Treaty

Imagine the aftermath of the Civil War as the Cherokee Nation signed a new treaty with the United States. This treaty required the Cherokee to free their slaves and offer them citizenship, marking a significant social change and impacting their land and political status.

1887: Dawes Act

Visualize the profound impact of the Dawes Act, which aimed to assimilate Native Americans by dividing tribal lands into individual allotments. For the Cherokee, this policy led to the loss of communal lands and the erosion of traditional ways of life, as land was sold off to non-Native settlers.

1900s: Resilience and Revival

1934: Indian Reorganization Act

Picture a new era of hope as the Indian Reorganization Act aimed to reverse some of the damage caused by previous policies. This act encouraged tribal self-government and the restoration of communal lands, allowing the Cherokee to rebuild their institutions and cultural practices.

1948: Cherokee Nation Reorganization

Imagine the Cherokee Nation reorganizing its government to better serve its people and preserve its sovereignty. This period marked a renewed focus on education, economic development, and cultural preservation, laying the groundwork for future progress.

1985: Wilma Mankiller Elected Principal Chief

Visualize the historic moment when Wilma Mankiller became the first female Principal Chief of the Cherokee Nation. Her leadership brought significant advancements in healthcare, education, and economic opportunities for the Cherokee people, inspiring future generations of leaders.

Appendix

1999: Cherokee Nation Constitution Revised

Picture the Cherokee Nation revising its constitution to reflect modern governance while honoring traditional values. This updated constitution strengthened the Cherokee Nation's government and reaffirmed its commitment to sovereignty and cultural preservation.

2000s to Present: Cultural Renaissance and Sovereignty

2007: Cherokee Language Immersion School Established

Imagine a classroom where children are speaking and learning exclusively in Cherokee. The establishment of the Cherokee Language Immersion School marked a significant effort to revitalize the Cherokee language and ensure its survival for future generations.

2019: Cherokee Nation Supreme Court Ruling

Visualize a landmark ruling by the Cherokee Nation Supreme Court that upheld the citizenship rights of the Cherokee Freedmen, descendants of African American slaves once owned by Cherokee members. This decision reinforced the values of equality and justice within the Cherokee Nation.

2020: Cherokee Nation Responds to COVID-19

Picture the Cherokee Nation mobilizing resources and efforts to protect its citizens during the COVID-19 pandemic. The response included public health initiatives, economic support, and cultural resilience, demonstrating the strength and unity of the Cherokee people in facing modern challenges.

Each event on this timeline is a chapter in the ongoing story of the Cherokee Nation. These moments of triumph, tragedy, adaptation, and resilience illustrate the enduring spirit and cultural richness of the Cherokee people. As you continue to learn and explore, remember that the history of the Cherokee

Appendix

is not just a series of dates and events, but a living legacy that continues to evolve and inspire.

Milton Keynes UK
Ingram Content Group UK Ltd.
UKHW021409081224
452111UK00008B/177